Marriage Is for Two

FAMILY LIFE EDUCATION BOOKS

By Frances Bruce Strain

Marriage Is for Two Men

A FORWARD LOOK AT
MARRIAGE IN TRANSITION

by

FRANCES BRUCE STRAIN

LONGMANS, GREEN AND CO.

NEW YORK · LONDON · TORONTO

1955

LONGMANS, GREEN AND CO., INC.
55 FIFTH AVENUE, NEW YORK 3

LONGMANS, GREEN AND CO. LTD.
6 & 7 CLIFFORD STREET, LONDON W 1

LONGMANS, GREEN AND CO.
20 CRANFIELD ROAD, TORONTO 16

MARRIAGE IS FOR TWO

COPYRIGHT © · 1955

BY FRANCES BRUCE STRAIN

PUBLISHED SIMULTANEOUSLY IN THE DOMINION OF CANADA BY
LONGMANS, GREEN AND CO., TORONTO

FIRST EDITION

LIBRARY OF CONGRESS CATALOG CARD NUMBER 55-11072

Printed in the United States of America

Contents

To

HELEN DAVISON LAMBERT

this book is dedicated in true affection

Chapter I

Marriage In Transition

MARRIAGE is rapidly taking on a new look in this mid-century and attracting considerable attention to itself. In *Marriage Is for Two* we shall take a look of our own at this new product of our time and see what it adds up to. Did I say, "Marriage is for two"? Marriage is for everyone.

To have styles in marriage, "here today, gone tomorrow," seems rather odd, but the changes taking place all over the country have not been so arbitrary as they have been sudden and unprepared for, due to the circumstances of the times—our military activities, the entrance of women into industry during wartime, our postwar economic prosperity, our freer social and dating customs, our one-generation family, our expanding educational system with its new racial equality. The whole situation is breaking down old traditions and building up new standards almost faster than they can be accepted readily.

There's woman's independent economic status; her industrial capacity developed so unquestionably that she can't be spared. Now that she has made a place for herself, married or unmarried, she is in demand and can find herself employment in almost any field. At first glance, husbands were not so sure that they liked the idea of a shifting of the marital balance by a money-making wife. "All right, take your job, earn your money, but don't forget me and the kids. And, just in case you should forget—you, in your blue jeans—I still wear the pants!"

But would these men, or others, even if they could, return to the era of the wife who had little to offer but childbearing and domestic service, who, old-world fashion, stood at her husband's side while he ate his solitary meal, and on a holiday or Sabbath outing, walked decorously a few paces behind him? Would any modern husband be willing to exchange his stimulating, companionable wife, with all her possibilities of helping to achieve their mutual aims and ambitions, for the weary, toil-worn wife of earlier days, just to preserve his "master" status?

Far from it. As a matter of fact, it is this man himself, with his new electronic, technological gadgets and appliances, who turned his wife "out of the kitchen" and into industry, into colleges and business opportunities, gave her the leisure to study, to learn, to earn, and to be his honored companion.

On the whole, men today are surprisingly proud of their wives' achievements, often aid and abet them, and, at times, take their places in the home routine. Last spring at a pre-Easter style show in a department store tearoom, the models were so unusually beautiful and gracious that a friend and I beckoned one of them to our table. "Tell us, who are you all? Do you have a special training course which gives you all your poise, lovely posture, and carriage?"

The model was amused. "Most of us are just mothers and housewives," she said. "What training we have we get battling with our young seven- and ten-year-olds—and our housekeeping."

"Who takes care of your children while you model?" we asked.

"They have lunch at school and we are home as soon as they are."

"And what do your husbands think of all this? Aren't they afraid you will disappear into Hollywood?" our inquisition continued.

The lovely model laughed again. "Fortunately, most of them urge us on. They find we are more contented at home when we have this complete change of scene. Besides, we watch our looks, and don't get careless. They like that too."

Another advantage to a husband is gained through his wife's outside activities—a new relationship to his children. Recently, I telephoned a young friend and was answered by her husband. "Connie's out doing precinct work," he said.

"And you are baby sitting, I suppose? How do you like it?"

"I like it fine. I'm the whole show when Mommie's away, but I'd rather have her here, of course."

Most men feel a bit forsaken when wives leave them

alone in the evening, but they take the opportunity of getting acquainted with their children and earning a place of their own in their affections. As mothers respond increasingly to outside calls, and fathers have a greater share in home responsibilities and the care of children, both the fathers and the children will be the richer.

Yet, for all its benefits, the change in the status of woman as it affects her home and family is one that still presents many situations for the united efforts of husbands and wives to solve. Not only has her domestic life undergone swift changes, but her social and sexual life has also. The pattern of a wife has become, in the transition, a custom-made affair. She has become her husband's personal companion, stimulating or comforting according to order, a sweetheart, reserved or demonstrative, always a participating sex partner, but ardent or conservative according to the nature and mood of the man of her choice. The husband, too, is moving closer, offering courage, sharing knowledge, giving love and devotion to his new helpmeet.

Perhaps the new and widening interests of wives outside their homes, the increasing association with a man-and-woman public, is a strong factor in the centering of a husband's claims on his wife in a personal, psychic, rather than a biologic fashion. She is to him first of all his wife, Jane. Second, she is the mother of his children and the maker of his home. And last, she is the woman who leaves for work downtown. This very personal claim of a husband may be his defense, the strengthening of his forces against the possible threat to his marriage and home which he fears her new business and social contacts can bring about. He still remembers the day when a man's wife did not lunch with another man or take plane trips with him or allow him to drive her to parties.

Today these are common occurrences. Everybody knows, now that the ladies have become annexed to business, that men and women have work to do together and with it more social moments will mingle. But the interest of both is focused upon the matter in hand, and nobody gives a thought to the fraternizing. Yet, with it all, husbands are husbands, and wives are wives, and both are cultivating closer, more individual, personal relationships, partly because of the greater sharing of each other with an expanding world, and partly because of the mutual interests that same world develops.

Friendly companionships between men and women are one of the accomplishments of the new social order today and add much of variety and interest to everyone, but their success depends upon each individual, his (or her) love for his mate and his adherence to moral tenets.

Members of the older generation, caught in this transitional period, do not always understand these modern ways, and speak their minds.

"It's all right, Mother," the daughter hushes and

comforts. "I'm not the least bit worried, so you mustn't be. Even if I were, your speaking to Sam wouldn't do the slightest good. Such things don't mean what they used to."

No, they don't, and parents' opinions don't either, after childhood days, partly because they are parents, and are to be emancipated from, and partly because most of them hold to the standards of their own day, as each generation does in turn. It would be difficult to convince most of them that of ninety and nine men and women who work together, only one (shall we hazard a guess?) goes astray. Because of the differences between generations, the preservation of parents must be one of the objectives of these swift-moving times.

One does not wish less variety, or to deprive men and women of the stimulation and pleasure which comes from broad association between them, but one could wish that it could have begun before, rather than after, marriage because of its great benefit to marriage stability.

NEW SOCIAL PATTERNS

The old-time chaperone disappeared so quietly that we have hardly missed her. Now and then at formals and such affairs she appears as hostess, but nobody worries much about her duties. As her successor, a democratic social pattern has come, known as social dating—the creation of the teen-agers themselves.

The virtue of the custom is the spontaneous association of boys and girls starting at early adolescence, which serves to develop insight, foresight, discrimination, and other qualities of mind through a wide variety of situations and a knowledge of a wide variety of feminine and masculine natures. In the gradual ascent through the first group-dating years to the engagement period, one phase of the whole custom, "going steady," has brought many to grief. Few boys and girls realize that the practice of restricting dating to one or two steadies during the high-school years is a significant factor in bringing about frequent teen-age marriages, many of which end in teen-age divorce. A high-school senior tells me that three of her eighteen-year-old friends have already been married and divorced.

The sequence is almost multigraphed in its repetition: a limited circle of young high schoolers, an available (but not preferred) boy and girl, immature personalities, a degree of what seems love and attraction, an opportunity or impulse to marry. "Why not? We can both work until we get started or one can work while the other goes to school."

All is done in good faith, but the structure is weak, and neither young person is mature enough to realize it. Sometimes the marriage breaks up almost at once. Sometimes the two hold together for several years. But growth and development overtake them, progress is not mutual, achievement comes to one and not to the other, and the marriage falls apart for lack of a common bond or because a new love has captured the heart of the progressive one.

Whether the teen-age marriage is the result of going steady and being unwilling to wait until "true love" comes, or whether it is the willingness of the girl to earn her share to finance an early marriage, whatever the reason, the teen-age marriage is one that requires a serious second thought, for it strikes at the foundation of the developing sexual powers and the maturing emotional nature. Another thing, these experiences leave a memory and the memory, filled as it must be with emotion and unhappiness, is a hurting one, so hurting that each such experience takes something with it that depletes the whole. Sometimes marriage itself is sacrificed and the person remains unwed. Early marriages used to solve the situation, when marriages held together, successful or not, because the young wives were financially dependent. Today, with economic independence, such marriages have little cohesion and divorce follows divorce with all of the injurious accompaniments.

Today's changes are bringing about other variations in the marriage scene—the realization of what we as a nation have held merely as an ideal, racial equality. A marriage institute in Los Angeles reports that for the first time in their history of twenty or more years young men and women of mixed races are applying to them for marriage counseling. Other such young people are attending study courses in college and a few are going ahead on their own with much more assurance than formerly. Differences between people, whether of race, creed, or color, are already being determined not so much by the degree of difference in their traits as by the personal qualities of each individual, as in the case of Mr. Ralph Bunche, and by familiarity with their background. A student on a college campus was recently heard to say, "If he were white, I'd like him for keeps,"—clearly, a recognition of the individual. Men who shared quarters with foreign troops in military service soon lost their racial prejudices, and missionaries who live in foreign lands accept the natives as they would their own compatriots. The unity within takes care of the duality without.

Our own answer to these modern perplexities is education, sex education and marriage education, which takes hold of young people as nothing else will and makes them stop and think. Yet, in spite of all, young men and women of today are keener than ever to enter marriage with foresight and wisdom. They want to make a go of it. They want to realize their ideals and have a family life that will be worth working and striving for. Those who go off the deep end, destroying their ideals with each tragic break-up, do not, we believe, act from intent but from the lack of the necessary knowledge that could point the way. This knowledge high-school and college classes, authoritative books, lectures, and magazine articles are supplying in greater and greater volume, and to greater and greater numbers—to young people who are facing marriage and to those others, married or unmarried, who, lacking this knowledge in their early years, will even more readily be able to take it to their hearts.

The chapters of this book are written for men and women of all ages who want to contribute to a saner, more intelligent approach to the lifelong union called marriage. For them are a few of the thoughts which observation, living, teaching, counseling have brought to the author of *Marriage Is for Two*. She hopes there is something in them for each person who reads them and who, having read, will feel within himself—marriage is for me.

Chapter II

Growth Stages of the Sexual Impulse

THERE is nothing among all of man's human endowments which means more to him than his sexual self, his libido, to use an all-inclusive term, nothing whose integrity is more essential to his married happiness. It lies deep within the core of him and around it the rest of him circles and has its being. It must be intact, uninjured.

Yet of all nature's children, men and women are the least favored in their sexual development, for in the government of the sexual impulse, man's laws and nature's laws have come into conflict. What should have been regulation became rejection. What should have been right became wrong. The inner resulting conflict is centuries old. Marriage suffers from it, to say nothing of the confusions and the mistakes it causes in youth. To understand these destructive conflicts and to fit our native sex inheritance into its rightful and acceptable place in modern life requires a knowledge of its laws and development.

Like the physical self, the sexual self grows in a fairly defined pattern with successive stages of development marked by characteristic activities and by a changing and enlarging horizon of love attachments.

11

The old loves are not, as some might think, cast aside. Who, at three, would ever forsake his mother for keeps in favor of a sand-pile buddy next door, or at twenty-three, forget her even though he was ready to take a wife? Mothers are mothers and they don't, or shouldn't, compete. The change is one of expansion, of reaching out and adding to, a shifting of the scenes to make room for new actors and, truthfully, at the marriage age, for a new leading actor.

The accompanying chart presents in outline the step-by-step unfolding of the sex impulse through the various stages of growth and change, from the nutritive period of infancy with mother as chief love, through the neuter period of the preschooler who adores everyone with equal abandon—everyone his own size belonging to his own world. Then follows, over a series of homosexual years, a period when boys are increasingly disdainful of girls and girls gang together for mutual aid and support. Puberty, or the beginning of biological maturing, swings the interest on into the final heterosexual stage when both sexes awaken to each other and intersexual attraction has begun.

The beginning of the growth pattern may come as a surprise, for few persons realize that the sex impulse, like the hunger impulse, starts with life itself. And, like the hunger impulse, it requires its own appropriate and special nourishment if it is to survive: mother's milk for the physical self, mother's love for the psychic self. Love, that is, is the first and last requirement of the whole, lifelong sex cycle. Reproduction is the climax, the peak achievement, but it is far from being the whole of the sexual life.

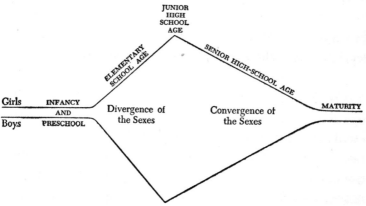

GROWTH CHART OF THE SEX IMPULSE

Note the slightly slower maturation of boys.

TABLE OF SEXUAL GROWTH

Age Levels	Psychic Levels	Love Objects
infancy	nutritive	self, mother
preschool	neuter	either sex
elementary	homosexual	same sex
junior high	transitional	both sexes
senior high	heterosexual	opposite sex
maturity	heterosexual	opposite sex

Because of the physical immaturity of children, almost all of their developing needs are on the psychic side. At the beginning of adolescence with its biological maturing the psychic forces merge with the biologic. From then on growth is but a perfecting, enriching, and deepening of those forces which are designed to find their fulfillment in love and marriage. How successfully and happily each person moves forward and attains his goal depends in a large part on the nature of his early growth patterns as they were influenced by home and community—how much denial and rejection, how much acceptance and nurture.

The traditional attitude of society for many a generation—yes, for centuries—has been one of varying degrees of rejection of the sexual forces. Built into a child's consciousness and continued through youth and maturity, repudiation and denial of a fundamental human need could not but bring about its own undoing. The misdemeanors (so-called) of childhood, the sex and correlated delinquencies of youth, the breakdowns of homes and marriages, the great numbers of mentally ill are today increasingly acknowledged as results of failure of society to recognize the sexual forces as part of the whole treasured human mechanism and to provide for their nurture and cultivation.

INFANCY

Memory does not go back to the early periods of infancy and childhood, but first impressions of acceptance and rejection can and do occur while mother and child are still in the hospital in the first week or two of a baby's life. The sucking, clasping, mouth-seeking activities of babies incident to the nursing period awaken them to the comforting human resources of mother and the satisfactions in reciprocal love. But harshness, withdrawal, rejection of babies, which is too often their lot, are carried over to them with frequent crippling effects upon their awakening inner psyche.

For various reasons many mothers do not breast-feed their babies and if a mother is disappointed over the sex of a baby—"I just can't face another boy" (or girl, as the case may be)—she may want to leave the baby in the hospital for a day or two under pretext of establishing a feeding formula. The disappointment is pretty keen on the part of the other children and a mother should think twice before she returns alone, but even if she does, back in the midst of her family, balance usually returns and soon she is calling for her baby who in no time at all will have won his own welcome.

Babies do not understand our attitudes, but they "sense" them, feel the rejection they indicate which often lasts into later years. Even delivering doctors, nurses, and midwives have not always been too gentle in pursuance of their services. Babies just emerging from the silent serenity of their prenatal environment have been frequently tossed and swung, slapped and buffeted in the struggle to catch their first breath of life, all on top of a rough passage down the birth canal. One wonders with what aftereffects.

For most babies, entrance into the world in this day of modern obstetrical equipment and practice is not the trying experience it was in the past and probably still is in the war-torn, poorly sheltered homes of Europe and Asia. Most babies suffer little permanent or serious harm from the experience of childbirth, and from most mothers love comes full and strong through the gentle pressure of their arms, the warmth of their bodies, the sound of their voices, their first communings—living spirit to living spirit.

So important are these first associations that many a modern hospital has fitted out private rooms for mother and baby together in order that no time may be lost in establishing the close mother-child relationship so necessary to a child's present and future psychic well-being.

√ Marriage studies show close linkage between marital adjustment and acceptance or rejection in infancy. The man who never knew mother love and care, who at most was merely tolerated, is not ready to give to another as one must in marriage. He is feverishly anxious to have another give to him. He is one of those men who see fulfillment in the older, maternal sort of woman. She is for him the mother recaptured. He craves her coddling, her petting and fluttering about. Although this sort of marriage is usually childless—how could it be otherwise, for children would spoil the mother-son relationship?—the husband calls his wife "Mommie" and she speaks of him as her "baby."

A similar mental mechanism operates in the case of the daughter of a wifeless father—wifeless in fact or in spirit—when the bond has been too close. "Why don't I marry?" a young and attractive girl of twenty-five asked. "I will when I can find someone as nice as my father. I'm spoiled." At twenty-seven, after her father's death, she did marry an older man who called her his "child-wife."

The laws of emotional development as they apply to the sex or love impulses, demand, if observations run true, that from the very first breath of life there shall be normal fulfillment with neither deprivation on the one hand or surfeit on the other at any of the expanding stages of development. Whenever there is, at any given level, either too much or too little of the required psychic satisfactions, inability to advance may occur and persist quite stubbornly. The child unwilling, yet helpless, finds himself marooned, imprisoned where he is, unable to progress to the next higher level. An adolescent may still be found to be in the preadolescent stage or even in the neuter or infancy stage no matter what the actual age or degree of general maturing. The sexually retarded person tends to remain retarded until the satisfactions of that period are attained. If infancy shortchanged me, infantile I will remain, biting my nails or sucking my thumb or going through any sort of mouth-seeking habits characteristic of the nutritional period. My cigarette, my pipe, my pencil tip, serve me as a kind of lingering evidence of the infantile pattern.

THE PRESCHOOL LEVEL

The second of the early periods of the love impulse, the neuter level, is a critical one for mother and child. Two related situations frequently arise which have direct bearing on later marriage happiness and permanence: the reluctance of a mother to give way to the first joy of her child's discovery of a contemporary playmate, and his reluctance to give way to a new baby in his mother's arms. The two situations are identical in reverse, and, if properly timed, each one fortunately can cancel out the other.

But if the mother has no second baby at her side and little son's or daughter's heart has gone next door to another little soulmate, she is likely to feel her supremacy is challenged. "Wait, you and Mommie will go down to the park and swing together." Yet park, Mommie, and swing do not make an adequate substitute for a playmate. The situation calls for park, Mommie, and playmate. In later years the protest is repeated: "What are you going to do about me, son, when you and Judy are married?"

But frequently the new baby arrives before older brother or sister has arrived at the point of reaching out for adventure. His interests are still mother-bound and psychic disturbances arise in him. There is a feeling of displacement, of being superseded and dethroned. Deep resentment can take root.

√Baby-timing (planned parenthood) is pretty important, psychologically, for both mothers and babies. Several tragic incidents come to mind: a three-year-old who flung himself downstairs after his mother's refusal to make a place for him on her lap during the new baby's bath—"Dickie, there isn't room—quick now, be a good boy and run away"; another who struggled to drop a log of wood from the fireplace into her baby brother's crib; another four-year-old who wrapped his sister's pet doll in a towel and pounded it to bits. All of these unresolved, forgotten episodes returned to leave the imprint of their being upon the texture of later marriage. We all know the frequency of the restless young husband who feels himself supplanted by his own child in his wife's arms or the jealous wife who cannot allow her husband to go on a business trip without her—"I'm coming too!"

√ In smaller numbers, there are those men and women who in childhood were trained to minimize sex distinctions, to treat boys and girls just alike. "There is no difference unless you make it." Such shadow-boxing, if one may call shadow-boxing denying a truth because it might hurt you, can carry the denial far beyond the period of caution intended and produce a greater difficulty than ever. "Man or girl, it doesn't make a bit of difference to me," a young man was heard to say. "I can have myself a good time with either." So can others, increasingly, as both men and women spend their days together in greater numbers professionally in industrial, recreational, and other situations. The question is whether the neutrality is the only basis of interest at all times or whether a normal heterosexual interest is also possible in its proper setting.

Commented a famous English author, Hugh Walpole, on our domestic scene, "It's a wonder to me that there is any sex attraction possible between men and women in America where boys and girls are reared together as one sex from the start." Perhaps this is our warning. Perhaps the entrance of women into industry may develop a sex neutrality at the cost of sex attraction. Personally, I think Mr. Hugh Walpole "had something," as the saying goes. Yet, interestingly enough, women in their dress styles appear to be using their arts to sustain and provide sex appeal lest it be lost in masculine garb. At the same time that women are wearing shirts, slacks, short hair, and low-heeled shoes, they are also wearing, in daytime as well as in the evening, backless, off-the-shoulder dresses, bright colors, much ornamentation, and rippling, swishing, flouncing skirts—the ultimate in femininity. What is this, if not an expression of the double aspects of woman's nature! Her desire to walk side by side with man, as well as to be enclosed in his arms.

PREADOLESCENCE

✓ The young preadolescents, just before entrance into their teens, probably suffer more from parental resistance to their sexual development than at any other earlier or later period. It is the interval between a nonfunctional, quiescent sexual status and an approaching functioning, active one that parents seek to prolong. It is the time, too, of a shifting of sex dominance, the casting off of female authority on the part of boys and the strengthening of male dominance—"Dad and I." In the case of little girls, it is the period of mother-identification—"We women!"

Unfortunately, the natural antagonisms between the sexes fostered by parental fears of approaching attraction gain occasional support from a man-hating teacher, herself still motivated by preadolescent dislikes. "What!" I overheard one such woman exclaim, when trying to cope with a mischief-making young ten-year-old. "What! Send that boy to the office and let those two males gang up on me? I'll take care of him myself!" Such sex bias is not often seen today and more men teachers could profitably enter the field of elementary-school education.

Occasionally one meets one of these preadolescent, sex-antagonistic persons who is an all-around misanthrope with no love for either man or woman. One of them served as a forewoman in a large industrial plant. She was skillful and just to her fellow employees, but she apparently loved no one and no one loved her. As a newborn baby she had been a disappointment to her parents. Her mother had promised her husband a son. When the baby turned out to be a daughter, her mother said, "She shall be a son, anyway," named her John, dressed her as a boy and cultivated in her boy's sports and interests. The girl was required to wear dresses at school, but changed back to boy's garb at home. When adolescence came, her mother wept. In her heart John was happy until she found she had no attraction for boys, nor they for her. Turning to girls, she found they too were unattracted to her. She was neither one thing nor the other. Because she could not love, she hated. She hated men because she could not attract them. She hated women because she should have been a woman and wasn't allowed to be. Her choice of employment in an industrial plant put the seal upon her pseudo masculinity.

One day she said, surprisingly, "I have a boy-friend. I wonder if he is going to ask me to marry him." What would marriage do to this woman? Would it soften her, heal some of the lifelong hurts, or would the antagonisms remain and her husband be the close-range victim of them? Certainly, before any marriage took place, there should be psychiatric help to resolve the old hostilities and, if possible, to bring about a re-education and adaptation to both men and women.

The love and hate expressions of childhood—"I love you!" "I hate you!"—are not to be taken too seriously.

They are a part of the emotional growth of children. But sex antagonisms and hostilities, cultivated by parents, can and do yield harmful results. A father standing in a doorway applauding his young son, who was blocking the path of a girl on her bicycle to the point of exasperation, called out: "Keep it up, son, keep it up. Let her know who's boss in this world!" A mother listening to the complaint of her daughter was heard to say, "If he ever steps out on you, step out on him and see how he likes it!" Yet parents do not always side with their own sex—"Look, son," said one mother, "you're letting that girl give you the run-around. Stand up for yourself. Girls are tricky. Remember that when you get married."

Where do parents get such sentiments if not from the smoldering embers of their own childhood? In some such fashion each generation passes on its own resentments, its hurts, its old injustices, its own unfulfilled desires. They filter through the welter of other affairs of the moment, a word here, a protest, a warning, caution, or command. The inner emerging sexual nature of each child stops to listen, is perhaps halted, temporarily, and goes on its way. But if the anti-sex commands and protests come too insistently, too frequently, then he may be halted permanently, unable to go forward to the next goal and on to maturity.

Those who suffer a blocking at this crucial period of change into adolescence have but little choice in the avenues of sex expression. Cut off from the opposite sex, either through the cultivation of their natural childhood antagonisms or through separation into girls' or boys' schools, or other maneuvers, homosexual trends already present in normal preadolescent sex preferences tend to remain and not only to remain, but to increase. Sex attraction for one's own kind is not the only solution, but it is one of the most common in the face of failure of normal heterosexual outlets. Instead of segregation at the beginning of adolescence, boys and girls should be given opportunity to mingle and to establish normal contacts and companionship. Boys' schools and girls' schools have much to offer before puberty, but leave much to be desired in social adjustment on the sex side after that point has been reached.

ADOLESCENCE

In adolescence the sexual forces formally and dramatically make their debut. The shifting of the scenes between childhood and maturity carries with it all that has gone before and the promise of all that is to come. It is both climax and beginning and holds a significance not present in the years of childhood just passed. This is the period of conscious memories. The influences and happenings are recalled happenings, not always active in consciousness, but ready, close at hand, muted as time goes on, sealed like scar tissue over old wounds.

Adolescence is not only the age of conscious memory, it is also the age of magnified responses. Life is more exciting, failures, disappointments, embarrassments more unendurable, joys, triumphs, successes more intoxicating. When, added to all of this, the thrill of sex attraction begins to stir, life presents a new and irresistible challenge not to be neglected. There is the first date, the first love note, the first kiss, the first repulse, the first double-cross, the first rage of jealousy, the first heartbreak of rejection.

These are the counterparts of the initiation rites of primitive peoples, their beatings, tortures, and scourgings, as the tribesmen go through elaborate and sometimes fatal rituals to test out the bravery and endurance of their youth before admitting them to the councils. But here the analogy ends, for modern civilization, unlike primitive society does not recognize the maturation of its youth, neither fosters nor tests out its capacities, certainly does not celebrate its final achievement of sexual maturity.

In our studies of marriage maladjustments and failures, one of the contributing causes most certainly lies within the American custom of cultivating delay in the recognition of and provision for heterosexual contacts and development among young people at their age of maturing. Yet at no time is this obligation on the part of society greater than in this period of early adolescence. The deterrent ideology lies in the long-mistaken concept of the pattern of sexual expression as it takes form in those first years of sexual growth. In spite of the startling and dramatic changes in stature attained at adolescence, nature's training in the ways of her children is cautious, ordered, and suited to their welfare. Attraction between the sexes is not the full-blown, emotional experience it is in the adult. Love is a delicate and transient bloom in adolescence. The kiss, the embrace are fugitive, uncertain, not always even pleasurable, the thrill often lost in the novelty of the performance. Yet love can be in its first awakening overwhelming and violent, even when it has neither depth nor permanence.

Yet lack of these exploratory activities caused by segregation at camp and school, long illness, family duties, infrequent social opportunities because of work or lack of funds—most of all, family prohibitions, discouragement by ridicule or over-protection—all of these may serve to bring about slackening of the tender awakening love forces, if not actual arrested development of them. On the other hand, more frequently today, prohibition results in forceful awakenings, clandestine companions, adventurous affairs, sexual involvements of various sorts far beyond the limits of personal need or desire. There are the scratches and bruises acquired among the sex brambles in an effort to find one tiny, longed-for bit of fruit.

How difficult is the course of man's sexual impulses when the laws and customs governing them run counter to the laws of nature and he must work in opposition to them; how satisfying his course if he were able to work with nature to conserve her laws and the well-being of her creatures.

The last of the three levels of preparation for marriage comes usually in late adolescence and the early twenties, or it may come at any age since marriage is not alone the experience of youth. But whether it comes early or late, satisfaction in some form at each stage of the love impulse in its unfolding cannot but count happily for what marriage later holds in store.

In the following chapters we shall look in detail at both the social and the psychic mechanisms that function to bring men and women together in favorable times and settings for happy, successful association. The odds of his childhood may be against him, but mischance, past or present, shall not, cannot destroy, even though it may injure, his own God-given right to love, marriage, and the gift of children. Marriage, however, is not for the weak. It is for the strong, for those who are willing to command intelligence, foresight, courage, endurance in its behalf and to fight for it, for it is life's finest possession.

Chapter III

Knowing One's Way Around

Social dating, the first of that succession of activities and their settings which prepare for marriage, is as American as baseball and operates in much the same fashion. You sit on the bleachers, an eager spectator for a season or two. Then you are moved to make a tryout. You make the grade, and, all togged out, you get into the game. Batting, running, you make first base. You try again, you make second. Third, you make a home run. The man, the girl, is yours.

Not all dates make home runs; at least, not at first. During the early teens, dating is largely occupational, "something to do"; recreational, "having fun"; social, "everyone is going"; and of course, sexual, but remotely, incidentally, first shyly, then matter-of-factly. Yet dating with all its accessories to be acquired— manners, dress, correct speech, social customs, called "knowing one's way around"—is not the requirement of the teen-ager alone just ready to spring into action with his crowd. It is the requirement of any person of any age who finds himself ready to marry but unqualified to make even a beginning at finding and winning the right person.

Look about you. It isn't difficult to identify numbers of marriageable men and women, academically, professionally equipped for the world of affairs, but babes-in-arms when it comes to knowledge of those subtle and often not too subtle attributes which can make or break in the end a marriage relationship or even keep a person from getting a fair start in the first place.

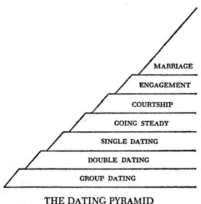

MARRIAGE

ENGAGEMENT

COURTSHIP

GOING STEADY

SINGLE DATING

DOUBLE DATING

GROUP DATING

THE DATING PYRAMID

The broader the basis on which one's social and sexual education rests and the more gradual the ascent up to the pinnacle of marriage, the greater are the chances of success when the times comes. Marriage is not a step to the right or left. Marriage is a climb, a peak to scale, challenging all your powers and all your wit in one glorious effort. You climb by stages, stopping along the way to make camp and record the log of your journey, benefiting by your experiences.

Many marriage experts have said, and we all agree in principle, marriage is what you make it. It is, but it is what you make it beforehand that counts quite as much as what you make it after the final "I do" is said at the altar. It is what you make it, all through the years of childhood while you are subject to home and community influences, as we know. It is also what you make it after you begin to date, to start the big adventure.

Group dating, going about in numbers, so secure and protective with its many skirts and coattails to cling to, is for the uninitiated of any age: for the woman-shy male or the reverse, a man-shy woman, for those who have been out of the running for any one of many reasons—illness, domestic or financial requirements, military services or training, absence from the homeland. And, among college students, there is that increasing kaleidoscope of those who come from dissimilar backgrounds, from the small town, the large city, as well as from Europe and the Orient—exchange students, refugees, all of them in a state of transition, all of them holding on with one hand to the past while reaching out with the other into the present and the future. For these two kinds of people, the belated and the transplanted alike, group dating, in either large or small numbers, gives the over-all view, lessens the feeling of the unfamiliar before the forming of those closer personal relationships that can hold one's destiny.

I recall an amusing situation arising from the meeting of the known and unknown that took place on a college campus some years ago. At an international conference one summer, the world of the East and the West mingled colorfully. The American men students, familiar with the free, open ways of the university co-ed, took the girls in stride—studied with them, borrowed their notebooks, smoked, dated, sat over coffee with them, as American custom permits.

But the new students from the Latin countries, accustomed to closely chaperoned girls, whistled and made passes until the American girls fled in terror, ganged together, and acted like scared rabbits in hunting season. But it didn't take long for internationalism to apply to social customs as well as to politics and trade, so that before the end of the conference all was well.

Another personal experience of the blending of the known and unknown bore a less happy ending. A young exchange student from one of the Asiatic countries visiting another of our college campuses had become good friends with a pretty, attractive American girl. She coached him in our ways, introduced him to her family and friends, acted as general mentor and guide. The relationship was close, romance was in the air. Then one evening the young man said quite casually in the beautiful English we all admire, "I should tell you, perhaps, that only friendship is possible [long 'o'] for us. In my country we are usually betrothed in infancy. My parents have already made the choice for me. I return to consummate the marriage."

There are, of course, hundreds of American men similarly situated, living abroad, but waiting to return to marry in their own homeland. One of them comes to mind who, after ten years, returned to his own midwestern home city. Ready to marry, but completely unfamiliar with the social scene, he dropped in upon one of a lecture series on marriage and family life. "I am thirty years old," he confided later. "And I've never had a date. How do I begin? I wouldn't know a sixteen-year-old American girl from a woman thirty-six!"

"Man alive! You aren't safe, you need a bodyguard in this country where everyone moves fast. When one like you comes on the horizon [he looked as though he had come straight from the president's chair of a Kimberly diamond mine or a Texas oil company] he has to watch out! Every sixteen-year-old girl will add ten years to her age and every available thirty-sixer will drop ten."

An hour later the young man was on his way in his shining red and black convertible armed with cautions and urgings to find himself a buddy who knew the ropes in good society and who would keep him out of entangling alliances for at least six months. There are plenty of lovely girls, there are plenty of girls who look lovely, but are on the make. One must know the difference.

It all sounded like an arbitrary assignment to a highly marriageable, upstanding young stranger who, woman-hungry, had obviously come back to civilization from isolation, wherever it was, to find his lady. Yet comfort was present in his general maturity which allowed him to be able to telescope his social education into a fraction of the time required for a youngster half his age.

These older men are tough rivals. They are more seasoned and usually have more money than younger men. They are more susceptible, too, to the sweet pretty young things than are those who know them better.

The story is told of a quaint little drama that involved a man in his early thirties. The girl was a charge of the juvenile court but was out on probation to her parents. Judge's orders forbade accepting an invitation to drive with any man unattended, or absence from home after ten o'clock at night. It was a stiff sentence.

At a high-school dance one evening, she spotted a personable young stranger and made her way to his side. "Could you tell me," she asked, "what time it is? I'm not allowed to be out after ten."

He consulted his watch. "Nine-thirty."

"Oh! Thank you." She was off like a fleeing Cinderella.

"Wait! I'll take you," he said. "Do you have a car?"

"The bus," she called back and disappeared.

The young man mused—early hours, no wild automobile rides, no truck with strangers—that was the girl for him. In a moment he was out in his Buick, chasing buses, found the right one, followed and met the child at her own door.

"Come in and meet Mother," she said and led the way.

The simple, sincere courtship was secretly probation-regulated and happy. Then came the moment of decision for the girl. Was a confession necessary if her whole future life would be good and true? She prayed. The mother pondered. Would the acknowledgment of a court record put an end to her child's happiness and this safe marriage? Conscience in both answered, "Tell all," and the confession was made. The shocked, bewildered young man listened to the story, faltered but a moment, then held out his arms to his weeping, penitent little bride-to-be.

Dating is a school of experience on the trail that leads to marriage. It is the art of personal relationships between the sexes along with modes and manners, including the art of discrimination and perception in the estimate of character and personality, the detection of the unreal from the real, the imitation from the genuine, the weighing of values both seen and unseen. These lessons are not easy to learn and sometimes our measurement of them fails, for there is no exactness in the art of human understanding.

Double and single dating often occur within the framework of the group. The daters share the protection and planning of the others, while enjoying the freedom of initiative and the closer personal contacts which everyone needs. "You get to know each other better." Yet freedom increases responsibility and the double date, as it moves out from the crowd to be on its own, often introduces a new factor, the tricky blind date, either man or woman. A blind date is an unpredictable person. He may be at one extreme, the wise guy, the four-flusher, seeking to crash into a new group after ejection from his own. Or he may be at the other extreme, the shy, untutored beginner, too timid or, like our "diamond" man, too unfamiliar and strange to find a date of his own.

The blind date is someone's responsibility. And that someone is the person who arranged the date for him. After that he wins or loses on his own. His lady may like him and he may date her again or he may fade away without further notice. Blind dates can be great fun and great finds. They may belong to another crowd or to no crowd or come from another city. But if they are "blind," without established credentials, they must expect to be subject to the full appraisal tactics acquired by experienced, often ruthless daters. They appraise his dress, his speech, his table manners. He belongs, he doesn't belong. They tear him apart, daisy-petal fashion.

Double dating often brings about an exchange of partners. The two men trade their dates temporarily for fun or, often, permanently. But in this exchange there must be mutual consent, all four agreeing, if old friends are still to remain old friends. I am reminded of a high-school crowd when the fellows arranged periodic "swapping" of their steadies without consent of the girls. They felt themselves pushed around and wondered whether the boys threw numbers into a hat and drew them out by blind chance. Incidentally, those wretches had the nerve to call their dates their "wives" and then leave them after high-school graduation to marry girls in other cities.

Single dating is a real step upward, carrying with it much fun and the extra responsibility of one's own and one's partner's entertainment. Money in his pocket is the man's first requirement, being appropriately dressed and ready on time are the girl's. But these are mere externals. The real contribution to a date lies in the flavor, the *esprit de corps* of the occasion, the ability to joke with the joker, debate with the debater, flirt with the flirt, quote poetry with the versifier or let him quote his own while you listen enraptured without a roving thought or fugitive eye. When it involves a different personality on each occasion, single dating has the stimulus of novelty. You may go to the same place at the same time, as you go to your favorite sunset lookout. You may eat the same food, dance the same dances to the same orchestra, but each experience is different. Time flies, or time drags. Money flies or money lasts. Different men, different girls, like different books, help the dater to refine a taste that serves as a basis for seasoned judgment.

But in America, alas, the tendency is toward going steady, a strange custom of dating one person exclusively without pledge of any sort—neither love nor permanence nor marriage. Yet it is a convenient, proprietary sort of affair, supposedly romantic to a degree, without obligation, though not without expectation, at least in the heart of the girl, who often cannot but silently nurture a faint hope or two that the steady date may change its spots and turn into a full roaring courtship.

Many a girl did unexpectedly get her man when World War II broke out and the men turned to those closest at hand regardless of the strength of the attachment. Many divorces followed, at war's end, for good dating partners are not always good marriage mates especially when the unions are based chiefly on expediency.

Yet, going steady has its points in preparation for marriage. It affords a close-up. It lifts a session of single dates, on and off with the same girl (or man), out of the special occasion, dress-up category and puts them both into the every-day just-as-you-are-class, unshaven or uncurled in slacks and sneakers, or off duty in fatigue dress or blue jeans, where each is revealed to the other with complete honesty of soul and display of human frailties.

The hazard of going steady lies in the break-up— probably in proportion to the extent of the petting and necking (whatever that indicates), always of more moment to a girl than to a man—and the possibility of the development of a sincere emotional attachment on one side and not on the other. Then, too, while one of them, man or girl, may be content to drift along without any commitments, other girls and other men with marriage potential are passing by and opportunities are forfeited.

We wonder how many steadies, percentage-wise, do marry each other in peacetime. We know how many married in wartime. But convenience, familiarity—"We ought to get along well together after all this time"—should not be a factor in choosing a wife. For shame on such lukewarmness! Why not make it a sure-enough full-blooded romance with your steady—or pass on to another?

To gain the value of the close-ups and prevent heart-aches, going steady should not be too steady. It could well be a succession of steadies, long enough in point of time to serve their purposes, but not long enough to create a possessiveness not intended, or to prevent the forming of later attachments.

Probably one of the most profitable lessons of the whole going-steady system lies in its unspoken code, which excludes the right of possessiveness. In going steady, you're on, you're off, but though there will be no hard words, nobody has promised not to care. To have had someone who is admittedly "yours," with whom you have spent the best of your waking thoughts and hours for weeks, months on end, even if only in a pseudo-engagement fashion, only to lose him, is tough going. In addition, if you've been taken into the heart of your steady's family and given the keys to the kingdom—in this case the car—then to pass out of the picture and see another in your old haunts, with your old steady, that is tougher still. But it is good discipline and may come in handy later on in marriage. Of course, if one or both were leaving to go off to college or to take a job or to go into military service, the transition (not the absence) takes care of the situation to some extent. A few ardent young steadies, not ready for change, talk about promises not to date while away, but that is an unfair request unless the steady relationship has turned into a sure-enough engagement and rivals have lost their sting. Yet even so, freedom is hard to yield, especially to possessiveness, which breeds and feeds on jealousy, chief destroyer of marriage happiness and peace. The only loyalty with any value is voluntary loyalty which requires no pledge of any sort. To give a pledge is to yield one's freedom and so spoil a spontaneous relationship.

In recognition of modern dating etiquette, a man who has been attracted to another man's steady customarily clears with him before he asks her for a date. One college man kept his eye on a girl most of his senior year. Time slipped by and graduation with departure closed in. When the affair looked as though it had reached its peak or, if anything, was on the decline, he sounded out her steady. "How about it? Is the dating season open by any chance from now on?"

"Sure, go ahead. It's all right with me." That was all, but it was an essential "all." Later, when the delayed romance got under way and ended in an engagement, the girl said, "Funny how 'cagey' you were all the time. I liked you, but I never even suspected—"

Another fellow might have played his game differently if two girls were involved. He meets them at a dance, shall we say, and is much attracted to one of them. But Finnie is going steady with perfect contentment. Elsa is not. Elsa is free. Dates with her would make possible seeing more of Finnie, keeping check on her, also possibly increasing his chances if and when the break-up came. This is a frequent, sometimes successful technique in the waiting game. But what about it? Is this really keeping a hands-off policy in regard to another man's girl? And what about the second girl who may or may not be aware that she is playing stooge, who may or may not become emotionally involved herself?

Double dating plays a double role in shifting one person to another person when a given attachment is not mutual. If the new combination yields a reciprocal attachment, all is well, but if one of them is hovering near to feast upon the presence of a beloved—hoped for, but not yet attained—somebody is not playing cricket. Yet so far as being "second choice" is concerned, if the truth were known, quite a few wives and husbands would learn that they were second choices or worse!

Two sisters' experience in being first and second choice all but broke up an entire family in modern Hollywood style. The girls were opposites—Frederika, dynamic, dark, talented; Frieda, the younger sister, blond, small, self-effacing, and maternal. Their young music teacher loved them both equally, he said, but differently, and hesitated between the two; hesitated a moment too long, for Frederika took over and goaded him into a declaration. Frightened at her own brashness, she made quick retreat, dated others more conspicuously than ever, and soon announced herself engaged to one of her following. Bewildered, hurt, resentful, the teacher turned to little sister, proposed, and was lovingly accepted. Quick reprisal followed. The self-styled "jilted girl" renewed her old attack, reviled, goaded, reproached, courted, made love, wept, and ended with a successful challenge to a runaway marriage. Such are the ways of womenkind (the primeval kind) under the handicap of the age-old requirement that gives choice of marriage partners to men, and to women the choice of acquiescence or the opposite, turbulent defiance, subterfuge, in gaining their husbands.

Yet no standard and no failure remains fixed. Not only are nations and peoples changing in relation to each other, but men and women are changing with an ever-narrowing gap between them, economically, socially, and matrimonially. In the attainment of this new relationship, there will be opposition, resentment, social clashes, and setbacks, but there will be progress.

For better understanding between men and women, between nations and the individuals who make them, nothing has been so far more effective than the study and practice of social dating. Better than diplomats, better than chaperones, better than laws and prohibitions, is this thoroughly democratic creation of our American young people, who will not let their institution suffer, even if, at times, it troubles us and goes beyond our ken.

Chapter IV

With Object Matrimony

COURTSHIP, compared to social dating and going steady is, as the old saying has it, "quite another dish of tea." The courtship period, whether between old steadies, taken unawares, or between comparative strangers (also taken unawares), or between fellow townsmen and schoolmates, is usually set to the quick heart-beating tempo of fife and drum. The casual, comfortable, see-you-tomorrow relationship of going steady is no more. Courtship "with object matrimony" admits no idling. You enter into it with sleeves rolled up and galluses taut. Then, too, behavior on both sides becomes more conventionally tailored. Men become more protectively masculine, women more dependently feminine. "I don't really *need* all this chivalry," one Amazon of a girl remarked, "but his hand under my elbow as we cross the street makes me feel delightfully helpless."

Courtship, even in these emancipated United States, involves, as one chastened and impatient lover profanely said, "the whole damn family." It also involves today a new type of woman who, while being all woman, is also a do-er, not a wait-er—one who goes after what she wants and meets a man halfway, if not three-quarters (or more). There are, though, still with us the maidenly maidens who use the same old delightful tactics of hide-and-seek, and some few who just hide-and-lose.

I remember some time ago, a one hundred per cent woman-conducted courtship. The girl was a magnificently endowed person fully six feet tall, if not more. Everything about her was as superior as her height which she scorned to demean by marrying a man shorter than she was. She was king-size; he must be likewise, or double king. One day he appeared on the scene, specifications intact, six feet four, a huge frame, good looking and, fortunately, easy-going, tolerant, and unattached. Hers was a whirlwind courtship, with her friends sitting on the sidelines praying, applauding, laying bets. In the end, a short engagement, an appropriate wedding to scale, which everyone was convinced held much of personal happiness for both. Yet some of us cast a forward glance to the children that might come of this union, for tallness is an inherited trait with not much chance of escaping when both parents contribute to the pattern. A more eugenic marriage would have been one between opposites in height, a short man in this case. That would not have appealed to this tall girl, but she would have had a chance at more nearly normally sized children.

There are today an increasing number of young

women who initiate and carry on courtship when the motive is less sympathetically supported by friends and society. To a local party recently, one of the town boys brought a visiting stranger. He danced and played around with all the girls impartially and politely. With one he struck fire. In a day or two he left for his home halfway across the continent. Almost before his plane landed in San Francisco, Denver was calling. Startled, he answered, "Oh, hello—what's up? Everybody all right?" "Oh yes, everybody's fine," an almost unknown girl's voice answered. "I just wanted to talk. Call me sometime and reverse the charges."

Sometimes it is not the young lady herself, but her father or mother who do the selecting and courting in the old-fashioned tradition but streamlined to modern ways. A young man tells me of a one-time steady of his who was accustomed to the best in places to dine and dance. He could afford only the most mediocre and dull. "Let's go to Father's pet place," the girl suggested one evening. "Do you mind? All the waiters know us there—we'll just initial the check and it will be all right." It sounded simple and reasonable enough —a generous, affluent father trying to lighten the load of a money-short young friend of his daughter's. Or was there a thought of marriage in the background somewhere and, if marriage, would there always be father setting the standard of living for his son-in-law's family? Many young men, like this one, reluctant to be an eternal debtor, would retire, taking their independence with them.

Another father was more successful at the beginning. "He was as nice as he was poor," this well-to-do father said afterward, and "though he and Barbara were not engaged, I wanted him for a son-in-law. I offered him a place in my business, gave him rapid advancement. After the engagement, I built them a house. He's a wonderful fellow, but the marriage didn't work out. I guess I did too much of the courting."

Fathers may also be hazards in an opposite, negative way. "He isn't good enough for her," they say, not realizing that in their eyes nobody will ever be "good enough" to break down their own inner resistance to giving up a daughter to another male creature. It is, I suppose, an unrecognized, or unacknowledged, possessive rivalry. "Do you ever feel like killing your prospective son-in-law?" asked one of them of another. "Mine is a fine, upstanding young fellow, but at times I could commit murder at the sight of him." He spoke lightly, but he meant it—in essence.

Mothers are perhaps even more difficult at times than fathers because they are not only mothers with a close relationship to their daughters, but women themselves. Every woman, we must bear in mind, is every other woman's rival, consciously or unconsciously during the earlier and indeterminate years (whatever they add up to). Young widows with half-grown daughters or young wives with older husbands would frequently be surprised to discover that they were craving a bit of contemporary male society for themselves, as well as, or perhaps, instead of, for their daughters. Such activities usually fail and drive young suitors away, for few men care to be railroaded into a marriage. Least of all do they care to be a bone of contention between mother and daughter. Yet a man who chooses a girl's mother first, and loses her, may count on her blessing should he be successful with the daughter (as President Cleveland was). But never can it be the other way around. A woman spurned would make a formidable mother-in-law.

More frequent are the matchmaking mammas who scare suitors away by promoting an engagement before the young people are ready, or those who are hostile to all young men, fearful of losing their daughters. One zealous matchmaker mother, anxious to get her daughter married off in spite of the girl's more than adequate attraction, frightened away one admirer after another by her promotional work. Telephone calls were intercepted, letters were opened and read to check the progress of the courtship. Then it was taken over personally on one pretext or another for direct negotiation.

Men are afraid of such managing mammas. Marriage is one situation in which they wish no unsought assistance. More than that, they know the outside managing will not stop with the marriage, but continue into later household affairs.

A young man who cared enough for his chosen one to accept the parental handicap accomplished much for future independence when he called upon his fiancée's mother to ask her formal consent to the engagement, already happily concluded. But this mother, who had been embarrassingly and unnecessarily active in promoting the love affair, abruptly turned into the bargaining parent. He must agree to several stipulations, she said, ticking them off on her fingers: "No domestic duties (going into the kitchen), no large family of children (to tie her down), no (by implication only) unnecessary marital relationships—complete freedom in every way."

Surprisingly, the young man was master of the situation. "My dear Mrs. Long," he said, "I shall endeavor to be a good husband. As for the details of our marriage, domestic or otherwise, you may rest assured they will be worked out amicably between us—your daughter and me." It was a good answer because it was honest and forthright, and had the desired effect of lessening future management.

Mothers hostile to all young men who wish to marry, or even to date their daughters are far more frequent than the mothers who try to high-pressure their daughters into marriage. The earning capacity of today's young women changes them from a liability to an asset.

"She won't let me leave her" is a frequent cry from employed girls who live at home. "She needs my help with expenses, so she treats everybody who comes so meanly they won't come again." Such a girl of legal age who is financially independent has the right to bargain. She must be assured of politeness to her dating friends or she will depart to some place where they will be properly treated. After such an avowal, painful as it may be (but need not be), most mothers will become more hospitable.

There is one thing to remember in this and similar situations: when the relationship between parents and children has been what it should have been up to the marriage age, full of confidence and trust, there is no reason to fear undue influence during the courtship period. Parents who have encouraged their children to make their own decisions will most certainly allow them to make them in so vital a situation as choosing a marriage partner. But if parents have been too managing in the past, a son (or daughter) may say to himself, "This is one time I make up my own mind!" Yet in most instances some expression of the parents' opinion is sought directly or indirectly. "Mother, why don't you invite Peg over to dinner some night soon? I'd like you and Dad to meet her." No parent is going to miss *that* opportunity.

Not only will children seek some expression from their parents concerning a prospective son- or daughter-in-law (often after the proposal and acceptance), but most of them would feel it a parent's duty to mention any circumstance which might be a deterrent—residence in a sanatarium for this or that serious chronic disease, a previous marriage or two on the part of an oldish suitor, the reputation of a fortune-hunting young widow.

In such or similar cases, parents have no choice, they must speak. They must speak objectively, laying all known facts side by side until they make a clear, logical picture without emotional overtones of bias and feeling. A parent who has the courage and honesty to speak out frankly must be listened to, the soundness of his reasons appraised, his facts and figures verified. Right or wrong, his opinion would be a parental obligation, and it might avert disaster. How much parental counsel shall weigh depends very much upon the qualification of the parent, his actual knowledge of the facts and his verification of them. In many instances where family feeling runs too strong for personal discussion, a skilled marriage counselor can be of real help in his objective, trained capacity in clarifying the vision of all concerned.

A young girl, shall we say, hypothetically (for there are hundreds in similar situations), has fallen in love with a handsome young stranger. Nobody knows him very well, his business connections are in a neighboring city, his family lives still farther away. "I know he loves me," the young girl confided to her roommate, "but Mother thinks he's an adventurer. How can I tell?"

"What makes her think he's an adventurer?"

"Oh, everything! He says 'I'm broke tonight, let's stay home and listen to some music,' or, 'Lend me a ten will you, that's a girl.' He breaks his dates (that I don't like), calls up from another town—'I'm going to be a little late'—and blows in at 10:30 or 11:00 o'clock smelling of smoke and liquor. Age? Oh, he's in his twenties—not in college now, but has been. He says he's saving to go back and finish—"

The telling of her story, point by point, episode by episode, like beads on a string, usually brings insight to a girl. In the telling, she is able to shift from the daughter of her parents, defending an unwelcome suitor, to a woman facing her erring lover demanding that if he wants her faith he must earn it.

We wonder. Was this an inadequate person, not able to work and succeed by his own efforts, or a four-flusher who allowed good looks and winning ways to do what hard work and application should do? Or do his late hours, shortness of funds, avoidance of public places, withdrawal from college indicate something even more culpable—a wife and family, perhaps, in another town?

In every case of this sort, it is to be hoped that parents will stand by, speaking generously and sympathetically of the young suitor and his handicaps. Although parents are theoretically on the sidelines today, they still serve as potent influences in the love affairs of their sons and daughters who usually recognize their rights deep in their hearts even when they pull away from them in the confusion of critical issues.

For those comparatively few young people whose families have always taken too dominant a part in all their affairs, separation and going away to school, or finding employment in another city is good business on general principles and can be accomplished without hard feeling. But emancipation from family, good policy as it is, carries a weight of responsibility for those young people who have delayed leaving home until the marriage age. They are not ready for the world at large, have but an immature basis of judgment and can readily fall victim to man-hunting, woman-hunting strangers. A young brother whose four older sisters kept him girl-shy, date-shy for years, walked straight into marriage a few months after leaving home. Expecting to find all women replicas of his beloved sisters, he was bitterly disillusioned. For safe passage you have to know where you are going. Marriage and guesswork collect taxes in heartaches and domestic troubles. Publicly sponsored lectures on marriage, counselling by recognized authorities, and books by established writers are first aids to the inexperienced.

In considering backgrounds and factors influencing

happy marriage, one hesitates to check off a list of requirements as one would in a recipe for a cake or in buying a new automobile. However, several prophetic surveys have been made with considerable accuracy and reliability.

Yet all of us agree that neither checking a list of personality traits nor knowledge of the way they were acquired through home influences, teachings, conditionings, experiences in the community, adds up to the expected answer. Vital as all of these tangibles and intangibles are in determining a person's responses and adaptability to marriage, it is the inner man's (or woman's) spirit, the psyche, unamenable to charting or weighting, to personal survey or questionnaire, that ultimately gives the answer.

A young woman who had dated comparatively little in her teens, had been subjected to much sex antagonism in her home, had no vestige of constructive sex knowledge, said "yes" to the first man who asked her to marry him, and made a completely happy wife and mother.

Contrariwise, a mature stock broker, who was looking for a wife, made an elaborate chart to evaluate the qualities of five selected women. On his sheet of graph paper he entered in a vertical column the names of all five, just as he had been accustomed to do with his stocks and bonds. Horizontally, he wrote in various desirable attributes: health, disposition, looks, financial status, companionability and, of course, sex appeal. At the bottom of the page he weighted each attribute, ranking health and financial status high since he had lost his first wife through illness and his own income through the depression, then plotted his curves. When the inventory was finished and the scores of the graph charted, he took them to show the winner with high optimism.

"It looks terribly efficient," she said with great seriousness, "but I don't see any wives there—not a wife!"

When he looked bewildered, she added, "Take me, for instance," pointing to her curve on the chart. "That's not me. It's not anybody. A person is not the sum of his parts. As an office manager you ought to know that. You have the chassis of a car here but you have no knowledge of its motor, the inner driving power, the dynamics of the woman, in this case. Besides," she added with a sly smile, "there is another little item you have left out that should be taken into account, warmth —ability to love. I'd tuck it in somewhere when you make your new copy. Otherwise you might lose your chances with all five."

In our United States, men and women marry for love. The marriage of convenience is not a recognized part of our social system. With young men and women today the core of marriage is the personal relationship of which love is the greatest motivating force, greater even than sex, which is only a part of the whole.

Two streams of human feeling meet in the emotion known as love. The first and oldest is the biologic, that deep-rooted drive toward reproducing one's own kind, the drive that is responsible in large part for the thousands of sudden marriages when men are called into military service. The second is the psychic, the mental and spiritual forces which come to flower, and, mingling with the biologic, make that nebulous, all-pervasive experience called mature love.

One of the chief concerns of young people in the courtship period is not that love shall be the basis of their marriage rather than other more recognizable qualities, but how shall they know when love—"true love"—takes possession of them, and how shall they know that it will endure and stand the test of life's daily storms and stresses, the hard knocks?

One must be honest. Much that passes for love is sex attraction, a good beginning but only a beginning. Sex attraction may awaken gradually and come later into full bloom. It may come suddenly and burst into an almost devastating flood of desire. It may come without one's will or against it. It may survive separation, or appear to be at an end, only to return when associations are revived. Yet sex attraction may not be complete even with sexual union, or shall I say it may be completed with union and leave no feeling of oneness in a psychic or spiritual sense? Sex union brings about a general feeling of bodily well-being and sense of peace—which is a biologic, not a psychic accomplishment, and it is not love.

In the association of young people together they soon learn (with heartaches, too often) to identify sex attraction for what it is. To mistake it for love would be to place a burden upon it which it was not prepared to carry.

The complementary element which brings completion and fulfillment to sex attraction is psychic attraction. It is the less spectacular, nebulous attachment, a oneness of heart and mind which can draw together even two strangers and hold them in defiance of outer circumstance. It is the quality which makes two natures fuse regardless of age or circumstance. When these two mysterious and awesome trends, sex and psychic attraction, meet and blend in a man and a woman, one may feel true love has been attained.

In everyday life, "the perfect love" is rarely met, if by perfect is meant biologic and psychic forces in complete balance. Usually one or the other element is in the lead, to lesser or greater degree. Men, generally speaking, have been considered to be more biologic than psychic in their sex attachments; women, more psychic than biologic. Yet there have been men, many of them, whose marriages have held together for a lifetime purely on the psychic basis. In other days, and even today to some extent, the two components of a marriage relationship were kept separate by social sanction, which decreed that woman's contribution should lie solely on the psychic side except in child-bearing.

Modern marriage based upon love is already making good progress in the enrichment of the ancient, long-established wedded state. When both partners, bound together by love of each other, home, and family, make mutual contributions to the marital relationship and find in it a symbol of inner and outer oneness, then marriage will give promise of the fulfillment of our hopes and our dreams.

Courtship is an effort to win the person who seems to be the embodiment of these hopes and dreams. Sometimes the ideal is found and sometimes it is not. More often we are satisfied to take "half a loaf," or we mistake the thrilling, exciting taste of romance for the substance of a deeper, more lasting attachment.

Courtship is a dress parade. The knights are in the saddle, the ladies are flaunting their colors, the battle is to the strong. Next comes the betrothal, the engagement, as we term it today, the final period of learning to know and of growing nearer to each other while preparing for the Great Day—the point of no return. Whether one's courtship will be the point of no return will depend upon the love of the two hearts involved, upon their religion, their home training, their traditions. It will depend, too, upon what will unfold along

the way, upon observation, discussion, taking counsel
from the experienced, from reading and talking—all
of the vast sources of today's surroundings which we
hope will awaken and clarify a few thoughts on the
engagement period.

Chapter V

The Testing Ground

FROM a man's standpoint, asking a girl the supreme four-word question must be an epochal event. Or perhaps the question is not asked. Perhaps, instead, he cables a message from mid-ocean to the girl of his choice, "FOUR WORDS," and she cables back to him in acceptance, "THREE LETTERS."

Because of the element of finality, asking a girl to marry you must be like signing up as a volunteer in the army. You can't turn back with honor. You are in for keeps. The situation is different for a woman. She can turn back, but usually she trusts her mind and heart more than a man trusts his, unless, of course, there are two suitors on their metaphorical knees and she is torn between the two. For a man, the multiple-choice phase is passed when he has reached the point of avowal. He has chosen his girl. He loves her. If she loves him, it is done.

Basic as this pattern of proposal and acceptance is, with the knowledge and awareness in one's heart long before it comes to expression (who invented the this-is-so-sudden idea, anyway?) variations are everywhere —those who wonder whether they ever should marry under the handicap of health, family obligations, or occupation (but often do); those who delay because of long-harbored inner sex distrusts and uncertainties; those who seek escape, adventure, financial support or prestige—all sorts of reasons.

Whatever the circumstance, under our social system when it comes to marriage and pledging for marriage a man wants to make his own decisions, his own avowal. He welcomes neither urging nor advice, prays only for an opportune moment, a lucky break which will land his girl in his arms without the need for a single word. "For the love of Mike!" exclaimed one desperately tongue-tied youth. "Do you have to spell it out for a girl before she knows what you mean?"

Yes, we told him, you do! Regardless of foreknowledge and favorable circumstance, a woman likes to be loved and won in no uncertain terms. The more unfavorable the circumstances, the better. In fact, she has even been guilty of building up hazards just to make sure a man knows his own mind and to hear the sweet, long-awaited words. Yet many a girl has lost her man just because he didn't know woman nature at courting time and mistook for genuine her hard-to-get play. A man who really wants his girl must take risks, must want her more than he wants to save his skin and come out whole in the skirmish.

I recall a young fellow who evidently in the past had been too impulsive in his proposals of marriage and had suffered too many rejections. Grown sensitive about what he called woman's "powers of exploitation" and not sensitive enough to interpret "straws-in-the-wind," he vowed himself a vow. From henceforth he would ask no woman to marry him who had not first given the assurance that she would accept him. "But why," asked the next object of his fancy after he had explained his position, "why should I risk my pride to save yours? So far as I am concerned, if men do the asking, they must take what they get. When women share the asking, they'll share the risks."

It's a Boston Tea Party deal, no taxation without representation. Yet there is something to say on both sides concerning this matter of saving face in marriage proposals. A woman is intuitive. She should be able to detect the trend and quality of a man's interest and keep it where she wants it to remain or direct it where she wants it to go. It's difficult, these days. A kiss used to spark the great event, but kisses are everybody's business today and don't count. But when there has been a period of devoted and steady courtship and a girl knows for sure that she can never love a man enough to marry him, it is both heartless and disillusioning for her to continue without giving her suitor some indication of her own state of mind. As in the instance of the man who "vowed the vow," such omission builds up a distrust of all women.

Yet on the other hand, when there is a genuine uncertainty in a woman's mind, she has the same rights a man has of continuing the period of dating without having to declare her position or to be accused of gathering "scalps at her belt" just for the fun of it. Because of woman's greater financial independence today and her ability to contribute to the expense of dating and courtship, even to the establishing of a home, she is already breaking away from her past reticences and beginning to assume considerable initiative in the business of making moves toward marriage, including the selection of a partner.

"Of course, we are not going to be stuffy and old-fashioned about anything," one of these financially established girls said to her struggling young lawyer fiancé. "When I ask you to take me out for an evening, it's on me. When you ask me, it's your party." Fortunately, social change takes place gradually, each one to his own liking. The girl who stood on her maidenly rights to be wooed and won at the risk of losing her man is giving way to the one who lends a helping hand. "You don't have to take it so hard," a girl said encouragingly as she looked into the face of her pale and anguished suitor. "It isn't so bad; speak up, Miles Standish."

Still more advanced are those ultra-modern girls who, catching sight of a man to their liking, lay quick plans for his capture. Surprisingly, the young man of today is not too resistant to the advances of an attractive and personable girl who uses adroit tactics. A socially well-endowed and financially well-equipped person of either sex is not lightly to be set aside. You think the idea is commercial and calculative? It would be, if on one side at least love were not in the making. As the old saying has it, love begets more love.

Yet if the truth be told, a woman-made marriage must hold a great deal if it is to be quite satisfying from the man's standpoint. At times it boomerangs tragically. A woman may get her man. He may have yielded his male prerogative of choice and be happy, but he does not yield it one hundred per cent. Deep inside he packs some of it away, unused, ready to call upon in time of need. "Who arranged this marriage in the first place, anyway?"

Oddly enough, when or if this marriage breaks, it is usually the wife, rather than the husband, who brings about its end. It is she who cannot bear the memory of her own handiwork. She cannot forget that, left to himself, her husband might not have chosen her, but another. Then comes the quick devastating thought: perhaps he already has another, a secret love. Fear, unfounded fear, tosses the fat straight into the fire. Under stress of suspicion and accusation, the husband asks, "Why the name if not the deed?" And "the deed" follows.

Such disruptions and the insecurities that cause them will tend to disappear when women have earned the right to share the privileges of marriage selection as they earned the right of political selection many years ago, so many years that the public has all but forgotten that woman suffrage has not always been. In the same way, eventually, the right of marriage proposal will come as part of the gradual social change which is taking place around us, with benefit to men and women alike. Not only will there be a sharing of the expenses of courtship and the engagement period, but much more important will be a lessening of the large numbers of women who have not had opportunities to marry, as well as of those who marry indiscriminately for fear of remaining forever unattached.

True, woman has always made her voice felt, subtly and intriguingly, if not openly. Yet women today are neither subtle nor intriguing. Education has taken away the need and given them instead ideas, purposes, intelligence, earning power, all over and above their still active endowments of domesticity, love of home, of husband, of children. If they remain true to their heritage and their education, they will make richer, more interesting, more desirable helpmeets. Men themselves will make richer, more desirable helpmeets, too. They will make better husbands, better fathers, be more flexible and understanding than they have been in the past.

So much for the "Who done it" in a marriage proposal. The next concern is who (or what) undoes it and who holds it intact through all the stresses and strains that arise during an engagement period?

Aside from the great mass of men who enter upon an engagement for the sake of marriage, there are those who do not intend to carry through. To them the betrothal is the thing. They crave only the advantages that an engagement brings—its companionship, its prestige, its escape from pursuing marriage-bound females, and to some extent, but only incidently, its light easy intimacies.

Usually the philanderer (if this is the name of a many-times engaged but never married person) is a most charming, often gifted man who is socially so insecure that he requires the support that a beautiful woman on his arm can give him, especially when she belongs to him and other men have no choice but to stand by silent with envy.

For the woman who for some reason is not free to marry, or who has beauty and not sophistication, or who lacks the required passport into a society that she craves, a brief alliance with an experienced tutor might have value. But for the girl who is looking toward marriage, the association must be short. Usually when hints begin to focus on wedding dates, the engagement somehow quietly dissolves.

Unlike courtship, the engagement period or betrothal should be of the garden variety of day-by-day association. Courtship is a contest. You are in to win and you give it your best. An engagement is a tryout. It is like the probation period of priests and nuns before they take their final vows. It affords, or should afford, a cross section of the worst and the best selves of the two marriage probationers, "For better for worse, for richer for poorer," with a taste of everything those words imply—a bit of bad temper (if temper there is) a glimpse of untidiness, (if untidiness there is) a bit of Sunday bestness and weekday laxness in every direction, just to make sure that the big strawberries are not all on top of the box.

As one young husband confessed, "I even tried to think how you would look when you were old and wrinkled." And another in a reminiscent mood said, "Do you know one of the reasons I was first attracted to you? I liked your voice. You didn't start shrilling in a crowded room." Returning the compliment, his wife rejoined, "I liked you because your shirts weren't too loud." One doesn't neglect leads like this. They have a value far beyond what meets the ear. They are the stuff of which marriages are made. The stuff that holds two persons together when greater factors fail—the livability of two persons under one roof, twenty-four hours a day as man and wife, smoothing rough places and healing wounds not otherwise bearable.

Livability is the quality of not getting on each other's nerves—not, for example, making scenes in public, not getting into a temper-tantrum when the paper boy misses the front porch, not calling for an accounting of every penny spent, not flirting (when it annoys) with every passing girl (or man), not scattering one's belongs on all the brand-new furniture.

Sometimes pride of ownership in a home of one's own, or setting an example to the children, or just becoming a good working member (which can apply to families as well as to office teams) will lessen or correct an annoying habit. Otherwise, new wives or husbands must accept old habits. Most persons know their weaknesses and sometimes marriage does inspire reform but not because of criticism or urgings, which usually increase the habits and undermine the relationship. Many a mother has said to a son's wife, "I don't know what you did to him. I never could get him to do that!" No? Perhaps it was the "not getting" that did the trick, the not "doing to him" that helped.

Beyond and back of livability are, of course, really vital issues that should be established before two persons marry—physical and mental health and ability to have a family. These are basic requirements which should and can be ascertained beyond question before marriage takes place, if it is to have a fair start.

What a young couple should do when these requirements are in question or obviously lacking is another matter. Each situation must be solved on its own merits and, happily, there are solutions. Health assurances for the future are growing better and better, thanks to the advancement of medical science and nutrition, though there is still alcoholism which medical skill alone cannot overcome, and there are a few inheritable diseases to give one pause. Most disturbing of all is an increasing tendency toward mental ill health. Deep as the bond may have become between two engaged persons, heartbreaking as renunciation would be, most young men and women would hesitate to marry and start a family if either were known to be suffering from a transmissable disease or an unsound mind.

Some time ago, I met a charming and highly educated young couple, soon to be married. The young man was blind. The young woman had been acting as reader for him in his college classes. But her own family carried a history of blindness of the inheritable type, she said, which made its appearance in middle life. Suitable as the marriage was in every other way the element of a common eye defect on both sides should have given this young couple pause. Yet all might be well. The young man's loss might have been congenital or accidental. The inheritance factor might not repeat itself. But, in behalf of children to follow (if they were to follow), there was an obligation to be informed and to be guided by intelligence as well as desire.

Histories of mental instabilities with repeated commitments to sanitariums and psychopathic hospitals come less readily to surface than physical ills. To most families, a period of confinement in a mental hospital is like doing a stretch in a penal institution and it becomes a closely guarded secret. Paradoxically, unlike physical ills, mental ills are largely underestimated by relatives and overlooked by the public which on the whole judges the passer-by rather superficially. "He's just an odd duck." Many persons suffering from definite mental diseases are filling business positions and officially caring for their families with no outward betrayal of an inward twist.

A very efficient private secretary, who would not provide meals for her family because she fancied that all food in her house was contaminated, had taught her children to go without breakfast, gave them money for a hearty lunch at school, and took them to a neighborhood eating place for dinner. Who would suspect a case of mental illness here, unless he knew of the attitude toward food? Even then, it would not be taken too seriously—"Just a crazy idea of hers." "She wants to get out of cooking." Many beautiful young girls and fine young men disappear and reappear after a sojourn in a mental hospital, or remain at large under curative treatment. They meet and attract others, fall in love, become engaged, with no word of the long interval of absence or the unsuspected psychiatric treatments. "Why should there be?" the family will ask. "Everything will be all right, after they are married."

One person in ten needs psychiatric help some time

in his life, we are told. State laws differ, but in California, at least, the law requires a seven-year wait for a husband (or wife) to be freed from a mate who has been committed to a mental institution. Is it too much to hope that the time will come when the legal requirements for marriage will include a complete medical and psychological history and examination before a marriage license is issued? Meanwhile each person about to marry must be his own conscience and represent himself just as he is with no unfavorable data withheld. As for the present, psychiatric help is available to everyone, usually with costs scaled to ability to pay. Today most cities have out-patient facilities staffed by competent physicians trained in the restoration of the mentally disturbed. Patients may also enter and leave hospitals voluntarily (after signing themselves "in and out,") though the seriously ill are usually committed by their "next of kin."

Whatever interest the public may show in behalf of marriage requirements for better physical and mental health, it is unlikely that sterility and frigidity will be included. Yet both of them are major factors in marriage happiness and performances. Both of them, too, are subject to help through skillful therapy. New medical assistance is forthcoming on the side of sterility and even more help on the side of frigidity, which is, of itself, rapidly vanishing as new emotional attitudes and new teachings are established in sex and marriage education. More and more young people are becoming voluntary and productive parents. More and more they are becoming voluntary, responsive partners in the marital relationship. They are becoming copartners and coparents in a very real way.

The other assurance, that babies would be welcome and a place be made for them, is fully as important as their conception and much easier to determine. "We don't want to start with a big house; we can always build on as the family grows" is a plain enough declaration for anyone and gives opportunity for the other member of the young couple to speak his or her mind.

Sometimes he does: "You forget, my love," one of these exceptions said recently, "I am not a family man. My work is very exacting. There will be much traveling and when there is I want you with me."

No babies! Just husband? Suppose a baby comes unexpectedly? This is the time to talk matters over carefully and arrive at some solution right here during the engagement period. Will husband be enough? Will wife be enough? The answers rest with the individuals. How much they hold for each other depends on their own personalities. They would have to hold a great deal.

As for the sex relationship in both the childless and child-blessed home, the same unity of feeling must inspire it that must inspire planning for a family. Both of these make the heart of marriage. Both of them maintain its unity. If procreation is the greatest act of the human mechanism, sexual love is the greatest expression of the human spirit. When sexual love awakens in a man and a woman for each other, they long to carry out nature's plan in unity of mind and body. It is as simple and awesome as that. Yet neither the expression of love or the act of procreation is simple or has been simple for many a generation. Man's protective laws of chastity and restraint, necessary for an orderly and humane world, have built up premarriage barriers which, while protecting the sex drives from misuse, frequently disturbed, even destroyed, the harmony of union after marriage. Frigidity in women, less frequent in men, has been the price of too long and misdirected childhood teaching. "Nice girls don't—" "Men don't like girls who—" have worked only too well and too often to the undoing of spontaneous and happy participation in the marriage situation. What has been pictured as wrong all one's developing years cannot be made right through the public sanction of a marriage ceremony.

A tragic incident of renunciation took place recently. A young lawyer who had seen at first hand much marital discord and divorce, fell in love with a beautiful girl, beautiful in every way. A quick courtship followed and an engagement, with strong possessive arms ready to enfold her. "No! No! I mustn't, I mustn't.

Please! Please!—" Each succeeding day the same cry, the same resistance. The young man's love foundered and his courage weakened. "No," he said, "I can't, I cannot face in my own family what I face every day in court. How do I know that she won't stay this way the rest of her life and remain the frigid wife like the rest of them?" In the days that followed, the broken-hearted girl explained, "I was fighting to keep him, for Mother always said no man marries a girl who is free and loose in her conduct beforehand."

Love-making during an engagement period is a perennial and major concern with most young people. How far do you go? they ask. The demands of an engagement today are both greater and less than they have been in the past. They are greater because the hazards and hindrances of premarital relationships have been considerably lessened. Contraceptives (not all of them too reliable) are available at most drugstores and other places, as everybody knows. The venereal diseases are subject to quick treatment. Chaperones are gone and automobiles are ready. One begins to feel all barriers are down. The demands, on the other hand, are actually less because the sex relationship (urgent as it may be between young lovers) is in itself only part of the kaleidoscope of two mutually awakened selves. The richer this psychic discovery the more readily the relationship is able to sustain a betrothal without the full expression of the sexual aspects.

Dr. Kinsey's studies reveal the higher the educational level the less the demand for direct sex experience. Yet American young people are not without their satisfactions. Love-making in all its various forms, from the petting activities of the young adolescent to the deeper, more prolonged love-making of the mature man and woman, has grown in practice, especially among those definitely pledged to each other. Its value in preparation for the marriage relationship and its contribution in revealing the sex tempo, or response, was formerly unrecognized. Now the frigid, fearful girl (or man) is revealed and a readjustment made possible before the tragedy of a thwarted and unhappy honeymoon and marriage.

The sex emotion has heights and depths as well as boundaries. Each person must learn his own pattern. Some are quick on the uptake, some slow, some ardent, some cool. Like cigarette-smoking, love-making runs over a wide range in practice and desire. With many, a package a day keeps the jitters away, but with others one puff (one kiss) and the chain starts. In sexual response, the chain is a three-linked affair, technically known as contrectation (petting and love-making), tumescence (bodily readiness for union), and detumescence (release and return to normal).

Women, girls, and children are strongly "contrectative." They are affectionate and happy with light caresses and embraces. Men are affectionate, too, but with the women they love, caress can pass quickly into tumescence, the second link of the approach to sexual union. However, sexual response is partly a matter of a mental set. You may set it on or off. An unattached man, ready for marriage, appraises all girls. The happily married man normally passes them by. If an engaged couple wish to observe the prevailing code of love-making without the sex relationship, it should be tacitly made clear at the outset of the engagement. Every person of experience, man and woman, has learned to know his own and his partner's limitations. It is a matter of courtesy and self-respect and consideration for the other person not to create a situation that will bring embarrassment and frustration, or the contrary, a breakdown of decision. Because women, more than men, are content with light love-making for long periods, theirs is the obligation to avoid disappointing and unfulfilled situations.

Like expectant mothers who face a long period of waiting before the great event, young engaged couples profit by engrossing and interesting occupations. Happy hours and days can be put in studying house plans, looking for building lots, learning to cook and to garden. One couple made their dream house in miniature all ready to hand over to the contractor. Another bought their lot and started building with their own hands. Holidays and Sundays found them both in jeans with pockets full of nails and carpenter's tools. Others, less creative, join young people's clubs, do volunteer work, or attend night school together, taking, possibly, courses in marriage and home-making. Still others enjoy reading aloud to each other, current or classic literature, which occasionally snowballs and attracts other engaged couples into a reading group.

One answer to the need for any substantial program for leisure hours is a not too long engagement period. Both the very short and the very long engagement hold strong possibilities of disruption. A marriage entered into after but a few weeks or a few months of acquaintance is a marriage between unknowns no matter how deeply they feel attached to each other. No person can know another well enough in two or three months to choose him for a life partner. On the other hand, the long engagement, one that goes on and on for years and years, often dies from ennui and old age. Its fires are exhausted. The spirit is gone, cold embers alone remain. In such a situation there is but one thing to do—recognize the situation and part amicably while still friends. Tragic at times, humiliating, but better than a marriage after love is dead.

There is another parting of the ways that has little to do with a too-long engagement; it rests on an inner uncertainty, even in the face of a true love relationship. "Is it right for me, an engineer, to take a delicately reared girl up into the rough mining camps of New Brunswick or the Canadian Rockies, or to some other place far from home and comforts?" The girl asks herself: "Am I ready to face the hardships with this man, or if children come, to put their interest first and remain behind in civilization while I send my husband back alone to his dams and bridges?" There are thousands of men and women today who must face the hazards and denials of a multitude of occupations in this technological age—aviation, deep-sea diving, munition testing. The decisions are not easy to make but they are easier to make before marriage than after it.

Personal factors, too, sometimes threaten an otherwise happy engagement and bring it to a close: A playboy attitude and a tendency to shirk responsibility, a great difference in age especially when the woman is older, a demand by one for the other to forsake his religion, objections and rudeness to one's parents, an explosive temper—all of these and many others have brought about estrangements and final breaks to once happy couples who loved each other.

Frequently, the two persons themselves feel, but cannnot explain, their changed state of mind. As uncertainty grows, it makes itself felt by a gradual edging away, a postponing of marriage plans, a reluctance to speak of the future, or, in those cases where one has grown cold, a failure to speak of love.

The gradually weakening bond between a man and woman who have cared deeply and later care no more is a tragic experience. Almost more than marriage itself with its down-to-earth realities, an engagement has held out the summit of life's aspirations, has beckoned one onward to its goal. There are, we know, hundreds of engagements, in name only, barren of the deep experience lying within a pledge to marry. But the breaking of an engagement that was genuine leaves a hurt that does not always heal. Yet for all this, and whatever the reason, when either of two pledged to each other seeks to withdraw or claim his freedom, it must be granted with good grace and sportsmanship.

Though a man is usually reluctant to desert a girl whom he has asked to marry him, it is a mistake to enter a lifelong union with inner reservations, an injustice if love has vanished or turned to someone else. Occasionally, it has happened that each had found another, and both were delaying the break out of consideration for each other.

Moreover, an engagement should be broken with some finesse, if not with gallantry. Persons under emotional stress can be unduly harsh and abrupt to cover their inner distress of mind. "It isn't that we broke up, it was the way we broke up!" many a girl has cried, and many a man has wanted to. Scenes with tears and reproaches are unhappy affairs with frequent outward yielding to reconciliation one does not want, just to bring an end to the storm.

Letters are sometimes more coherent than speech, in ending an engagement, and are far more easily delivered. From sheer lack of courage, many an escaping lover has managed to get himself transferred to another business location, or a girl has persuaded her parents to send her to Europe or some other distant place, "just to make sure," she will say, in explanation. Yet everyone knows, if love is as sure and strong as it should be before marriage, no absenteeism is required to make assurance doubly sure.

A season of broken engagements among one's friends like a season of broken marriages (they really are contagious) gives one pause and precipitates a fever of pessimism. "I think I'll stay single." "Me for bachelorhood." Yet pessimism is not warranted. The world is full of happily married couples who have surmounted unbelievably rough places and surmounted them purely through love and emotional balance, the two strongest assurances of marriage permanence. Rough places do not break up an engagement, but lack of love and impulsive rough speech and conduct do.

Today the scene looks brighter with boys and girls growing up together from childhood free from the sex fears and biases of other days, with spontaneous dating permitted from early adolescence, a certain amount of light petting recognized as a normal activity along with teen-age love affairs, and college classes and church forums ready with programs to guide them for the future—with all of this one may look forward to surer, happier engagement days.

In a word, an engagement to marry is a testing, not so much a weighing and selecting as a revealing of two inner personalities in all possible human and psychic ways. It is a season of growth, of discovery stimulated by the interplay of a man and a woman inspired by love, confidence, and joy, who are preparing for the great adventure of marriage.

Chapter VI

Honeymoon and Home

OCCASIONALLY you hear someone say of two old friends, "Their marriage has been one long honeymoon," or, "They've been married over a dozen years and never had a difference." Is this something to applaud? Is it desirable always to be in agreement? Or do you want to be a challenge to each other? Variety, not monotony (which often spells monopoly), sets a surer basis for growth and contentment.

When marriage remains a honeymoon, when after twenty years a husband is still calling his childless wife his bride, when another treats his like a motion-picture star, or one of them "yeses" the other so habitually that he ends by teasingly but pointedly, bestowing a nickname—"Yes-Madame" (Yes-Madame's birthday, Yes-Madame's garden, or whatever) something is likely to be wrong. These people are going through the motions and the marriage itself is marking time.

Marriage, to be marriage, must grow. It must grow as a business grows when two partners have invested their life savings in a united venture. They keep books. They know at the start there will be items on both sides of the ledger. Sometimes they will find themselves in the red. There will have been poor judgment, misundertandings, quarrels. But there will be increasingly long stretches when they will be in the black, when both have learned to pull together, when confidence in each other has been established and they are more and more frequently seeing "eye to eye." This is the way a business partnership becomes stabilized. It is the way a marriage develops and becomes stabilized. We know and expect a period of transition before it becomes a working concern. But in marriage, we also know, there is an element that is not present in business, a special relationship, a love relationship that sharpens every issue and influences its outcome and its solution.

Although the contract of the partnership "Mr. and Mrs." goes into effect at the altar, the opening days, the "At Homes" are usually postponed until after the honeymoon, that period sometimes termed "the vestibule" of married life. But if, in search of realities, a honeymoon is not to be prolonged into marriage, like overripe fruit, let marriage be absorbed into the honeymoon. Hosts of bridal couples today go no farther on their wedding journey than they are able to drive for a weekend and return by Monday, ready to go to work and to housekeeping. This sort of honeymoon, it seems to me, has many advantages over the traditional one staged with secrecy and obscurity, far removed from the customary affairs of daily life.

Although the bride and her family bear the expense

of the wedding, the cost of the honeymoon, to say nothing of gifts to the best man, the ushers, the fee to the clergyman, falls to the bridegroom together with the major expense of establishing a home. It is all quite staggering to a young man who must rely on his own resources, even if he happens to have welcome cash wedding gifts.

A well-to-do relative of a small-salaried young fellow wrote a generous check for his wedding gift, tentatively earmarked for some of the furnishing of his new home. "Let's use it for a bang-up honeymoon," the happy bridegroom cried "We'll only be married once!" In two weeks they were back home, with the bride carried over the doorsill and set down upon a kitchen chair in the center of a stone-bare room.

"But we had fun," they said, "swimming, lying on the beach, soaking up the sun, dining on lobster and crab, and dancing to wonderful bands." Yes, they had fun, but does a newly married couple need the glamour and night life of a swank resort hotel to enhance their honeymoon? Would there have been no "fun" in shopping together for their first home and standing in the doorway welcoming the big delivery van as it drove up to disgorge the new furnishings which they together settled into place?

Honeymoon extravagances are forgivable and tempered wedding pageantry even recommended. In this streamlined age we need the interlude of a peace-filled holy moment, such a moment as a few of us shared recently in a small but beautiful Gothic chapel unadorned except for an altar arrangement of white lilies.

But honeymoons! When the stage is set for two, and the rest of the world well lost, why sacrifice essentials to keep in its midst? Is a girl not likely to stop and wonder if this man of hers is always going to be an impulsive spender, rich one day, poor the next? A thrifty man must also wonder if his girl is always going to overspend or will she settle down and learn to stretch his dollars, watch for specials at the markets, and for sales at the department stores?

A girl's attitude during her engagement, especially toward the purchase of an engagement ring, is a pretty sure index of her sense of values. "I'm afraid I can't compete with this," a newly accepted suitor lamented, ruefully indicating the large diamond his lady was wearing on her right hand. "You don't need to," she answered. "That's a graduation gift from my father. I couldn't part with that and two solitaires are too many. Let's wait for the wedding ring." Remember there is a wedding ring coming up after a while which can have a few sparklers, if you wish.

Too much emphasis has been laid upon the formality of an announcement and the place the engagement ring plays in it. Even wedding plans frequently are held up until the ring is produced, often at the cost of living essentials, proper food, rest, and clothing. A man works overtime to buy his girl a ring when the lack of it is all that stands between having her now or later. But should he, and should she allow him to?

A young girl who found out that her sweetheart was doing without his summer vacation in order to buy her a diamond ring soon took care of that matter. What did he think she wanted, a silly ring or a nice strong husband? As a matter of fact, a lot of silly rings from ten-cent stores and novelty shops are being given in fun when the cost of a valuable diamond is out of the question. There is also the old family box of heirloom jewelry to draw upon. And of course the very acceptable fraternity pin or ring which answers all requirements. Every man can contrive something even if he has to join a class in art metalwork at the local Y.M.C.A.! With most girls, the value of an engagement ring is not the first consideration. She just wants something to show, some visible symbol of her new status.

As for the honeymoon, it is today much more of a tradition than the necessity it was considered when it served the unhappy purpose of initiating untutored brides into the mysteries of wifehood, a procedure which wrecked many a marriage before it had begun. As young people today become intelligently educated in the essential aspects of the marriage relationship through their high-school and college courses, the purpose of the honeymoon changes. It becomes a joint vacation, freer, less urgent, with surer promise of happy memories.

Yet, even today our young people are not sex-educated, or marriage-educated. Tensions and anxieties are still among them, heightened, as the honeymoon approaches, with quite as much insecurity on the part of the young groom as on the part of the bride. After all, this is his hour. He is the leading man. For those continent bridegrooms who have set up fixed and substitute patterns of sexual release or expression and held to them during the premarriage years, the sudden change into the marriage relationship is not always readily achieved. Old patterns tend to persist and a man may require time, a relaxed mind and freedom from urgency and self-consciousness, to be able to shift over to the new requirements of a husband. Even if a bridegroom is not inhibited, but happily ready to consummate his marriage, his lady may not be. She too, may be inhibited by old resistances, old "touch-me-not" teachings, old modesties which hamper her freedom and make beginnings difficult.

With the possibility of some variation in these all too frequent situations, a honeymoon in a strange place—hotel, camp, plane, and where-not, among crowds and vacation travelers—seems the least desirable of choices. Or there's the opposite: a secluded spot, with few diversions, twenty-four-hour-a-day unbroken companionship, over-concentration on sex adjustment, possible embarrassment over ineptitude, even tears, self-reproaches, and accusations. These possibilities would suggest a not too remote and isolated retreat for any but the most sophisticated and assured. But for those who are not, how much more satisfying and reassuring would be working out their mutual adjustments at home, after a short holiday, unpacking wedding gifts, getting settled, spending daytime hours apart, evenings working together in house and garden, nights loving and talking and sleeping with the sex element fitting itself spontaneously and naturally into the whole domestic scene.

A young husband, now the father of several children relates how an unexpected telegram arriving on the third day of a most discouraging honeymoon was a life-saver for him. Returning to the honeymoon retreat after a day or two away, in response to the wire, he was entirely in command of the situation, his confidence restored, his fears dispelled. The break, the occupation with the routine affairs of life, had given him the breather that he needed and all was well. Like engagement rings, honeymoons should not be required, but fit into the circumstances and the needs of both persons involved. Then it may truly be enjoyed both in prospect and in retrospect.

Sometimes the choice of a honeymoon location can be the start of a marriage rift. At a bridal shower, a short time ago, a happy, excited girl was chatting gaily about her future. "We are sure to get along well," she said. "Chuck and I like the same things. He likes the out-of-doors, especially camping, sailing, hiking, but he doesn't care for the ocean as I do. That's because he was brought up in the lake country. He doesn't know anything about the ocean. But he will— we are going to Atlantic City on our honeymoon."

What was she going to do with a fresh-water person in Atlantic City, someone wondered. Oh, he could sit out on the piers and watch the breakers, or amuse himself on the boardwalk if he didn't want to try the water with her.

Woman, woman! She'd better watch her own breakers! Atlantic City boardwalks, tourists, did not add up to either recreation or a honeymoon for a vigorous sports-loving man. It looked like a bad beginning. How long will the ego of some women put their men to the test as soon as they have them, and how long will men let them?

Independent decisions which start during the first weeks of marriage are likely to become the rule. In domestic matters, women are expected to take command and husbands are glad to have them so far as operation is concerned. But plans must include him in a very special way, for home is a refuge, a place for rest, relaxation, and enjoyment—a place in which to drop one's worries and find renewal of mind and body. But husbands are not always borne in mind, and are often too modest to say in a neglected moment, "Hi, don't forget me!"

One of these self-effacing men, who had just built a new modern house for his family, was showing an old friend around the beautiful rooms at a house-warm-ing. "Yes," he said, "it is about perfect in Estelle's eyes. But I miss my old bed."

"Your bed? Where is it?"

"Down in the storeroom. Estelle felt it was out of place among all these modern things—too old-fashioned." Couldn't he sneak it up into his own room some time and keep the door closed, we suggested, for there was Estelle's own separate room and bath far down the hall. He didn't think that would do. It would make trouble, he thought, The bed didn't really matter after all, for you slept all the time you were in it anyway.

These are the men who spoil their wives, lose their love, and mess up their own lives, if not their marriages. "Why doesn't he stand up for his rights?" a spoiled little wife asked. "I'd think more of him if he did!" You have only to look about you to see this situation repeated in your own circle of friends. Fortunately, there are not many, proportionately, of these women, but there are too many one-sided lifelong devotions. The same absorption of one by the other occurs when the wife is the sacrificed one. We all know the elderly invalid woman, who regains her health, "blossoms out," and renews her youth after her too-devoted husband has gone.

In many instances, a meager childhood is found in the dominant one. Children who have been greatly restricted from childhood need, for their rounded development, freedom to think, to act, to make mistakes, to learn, to question, to make decisions on their own. When these have been denied, there is little left in adulthood to give to a wife or a husband in marriage. One cannot give before he has received. Yet there are many young couples who, after a normal free and happy childhood, are capable of both giving and receiving in balanced proportions. Such a mutual assistance league must be set up during the engagement period, if it is to be in working order for marriage. After the wedding, other adjustments will be crowding to the fore. In their joy in each other and in the glow of early love, indulgence comes easily to young marrieds. What do trifles matter? But time tells. Softness, sweetness, weakness are as fatal to family growth and contentment as are perversity, selfishness, and dominance. In fact, they are usually found together, aiding and abetting each other. Sweetness aids perversity, unselfishness aids selfishness, weakness aids dominance.

"Giving in," turning the other cheek, bargaining ("It's my turn!"), all are makeshifts because they leave the inner situation unchanged. A young wife said, "Yes, I gave in because something was going to break if I didn't." That is not even compromise. That is sandbagging, holding your finger in the dike to prevent immediate disaster. Husbands and wives must care enough to want to see each other's point of view and to make the other's happiness and welfare his own. Selfishness cannot develop under such mutual thought for each other, for neither will let unselfishness be imposed upon. Neither is monitoring for himself. Each is lobbying for the other.

You know the old saying, "If you take care of the pennies, the dollars take care of themselves." In marriage, if you take care of the little things (like beds and blankets) there won't be any big things to worry about. But instead, like children, we are apt to eye each other's candy bar, exaggerate differences, become resentful, exchange sharp words until, as one wit phrased it, domestic life becomes a "disputatious forum."

Although usually disputes do not solve personal difficulties, they sometimes clear the air and bring to the surface underlying causes of ill-feeling. "I don't know what's the matter with her," a hundred and one husbands say. "I'm just in the doghouse, that's all I know." Whereas their wives will say, "He won't talk! How are we going to get together if he clams up and won't talk to me!"

Talking over a difference should help if both people genuinely want to see each other's point of view. But there is such a thing as talking so long and so much that you talk yourself out of your troubles and back into them again. "I'm sorry I didn't realize—" begins like an apology and the person who doesn't stop to listen to it is considered ungracious and ill-bred. But often the "I'm sorry" turns into another onslaught which widens the breach instead of closing it. You may not apologize and throw stones at the same time.

Much talking is also likely to open up a rehearsal of old scores which (one thought) had been long since erased, but now are recalled to increase the bulk of accusations.

It would be futile to mention and discuss the hundreds of minor points of domestic irritation when two persons of different backgrounds, habits, and standards come together to establish a home. Many of the causes go back to fundamentals lying within all human beings.

1. We dislike giving up our adult personal freedom. (We want to do as we please in our own house.)
2. We harbor disproportionate concern over trifles. (Men discount the trifles women value. Women discount the trifles men value.)
3. We resort to small annoyances as substitutes for attacks of greater import.
   (Give backhanded compliments in public)

But when love is strong and each one cares, the small annoyances fade away. One modifies some of his bothersome pet habits, the other does a bit of indulging. But neither feels required to yield all of his personal freedom, nor encroach upon the personal freedom of the other. One devoted wife gathered up the scattered pages of several metropolitan newspapers every day from her living-room floor. "I know I shouldn't throw those things all over the place," her husband confessed, "but I want to! I like the feeling—the spread-out feeling." Fortunately, his wife understood. "He makes it up to me in other ways," she explained. "Anyway, why shouldn't he? It's his little fling!"

As a matter of fact, a sense of order about personal belongings appears to be a variable within wide limits. A gift of the gods, it is subject to easy or difficult training with orderly minds not always associated with orderly bureau or desk drawers, and orderly drawers not always with orderly minds. Yet, parents often find that a tidyness which had not been apparent in early childhood was achieved later under the strong motivation of a home of one's own or the requirements of office or laboratory. Said a young teen-ager: "When I have a place of my own I'm going to have a card catalogue of everything in the house!" "It will take more than a card catalogue," we told him and thought the card catalogue not a bad idea. Followed through, it might help find a permanent home for displaced articles.

Punctuality should be the twin brother of orderliness, but it isn't; a strictly orderly person may be strictly unpunctual. Ten-thirty may be ten-forty. It is a pity, for the time a person saves being orderly, he loses by being behind time. Lateness to meals, lateness in catching trains, in keeping and meeting domestic engagements are each enemies to domestic peace and makers of frayed nerves. Women who see their carefully prepared dinners getting cold and unpalatable while the clock ticks off the quarter, half, three-quarter hour, are torn between fear for their husbands' safety and their righteous indignation over a spoiled meal and hungry, fretting children.

One wife relates that she warmed over, or prepared two dinners, for a week, thinking that her husband was detained at the office on business, only to find out quite accidentally that he had been stopping to watch a golf marathon which was in full swing at a country club he passed each evening on his way from work. Why do husbands tax their wives' patience by being late to meals, or bringing home unexpected guests, or not coming at all without notification when a telephone call would ease the whole situation and be common courtesy besides? There is also the person who becomes so absorbed in his work, time gets away from him and he misses trains and planes with abandon. "I'm sorry, I was just trying to finish—" Punctuality is a habit and can be acquired for the sake of general workability and livability with others. Yet punctuality can also be a fetish when all other issues are lost sight of, and even made to suffer, just in behalf of "being on time." Punctuality is not a creed. It is a human device for smooth community operation and should be used to that end. When it isn't, and instead makes everyone unhappy, it should be set aside. We have not spoken of the unpunctual wife who keeps her hungry family waiting for meals, for that would be assailing her whole domestic competence, which in each case is different. Yet, recently, a young husband was granted a divorce solely on the basis of domestic neglect. He was tired, he said, of coming home at night to unmade beds, unwashed dishes, overflowing laundry baskets, undarned socks, and unprepared meals.

"Does your wife work?" asked the judge.

"At nothing!" answered the husband.

"Divorce granted," said the judge.

Getting a procrastinating husband and family of children off on their vacations is as nothing to most wives who have had the experience of leaving a husband at home for a summer to carry on alone until he can join them and escort them home. "It wasn't the stacks of unwashed dishes, empty bottles, weekly laundry that I knew were collecting," said one dejected wife. "I expected those, but I didn't expect he'd tear the house apart and splash buckets of paint over everything. Look at my house!"

A few cans of paint in the garage, a few brushes, a hammer and a few nails, and the lonely husband turns boy one hundred per cent with no veto power at hand. The average man does not think in terms of shades and colors. He doesn't know how long a decorator takes to mix wall paints to the exact shade that will harmonize with rugs and draperies. He doesn't know that bathrooms have a special "decor" of their own in equipment and furnishings. He only knows time hangs heavy and he has a yen "to freshen up the house."

Another lonely husband after two days in his own kitchen, took inventory of its content, plotted "efficiency" changes, and rearranged the entire setup, including small wall gadgets such as towel racks, can openers, orange squeezers, and the rest. Homecoming brought a storm of protest. Why couldn't he have said something, before he reorganized her kitchen? his wife moaned. She wouldn't molest his office, not even his closet or bureau drawers. No, a good wife wouldn't. In every house there are personal spots which the other leaves to its owner. A woman's kitchen is one of these spots. A man's desk, his toolbox, the "junk" in the garage are supposedly sacrosanct. The house and garden or yard is common property and because it is, drastic changes must be worked out in common. These are not fixed items or clauses such as one might include in a written contract. Husbands and wives don't operate that way. Marriage operates by tacit agreement, by knowing each other's requirements, likes, and dislikes and observing them.

As for vacationing together, that is a matter of individual choice and circumstance. "Our lives are so full, I scarcely see my husband except on vacations," speaks for itself. Yet there are other situations when everybody would benefit by independent jaunts—the wife visits her family, the husband visits his. During the work year, there are always those national conventions coming along—Masonic, Legionary—which would give the husband just what he needs. But that would mean going by himself, for how could he dress up, step up, and cut up if his wife were there? These urgings do not last forever. In a few years most fathers are ready to omit conventions and in summer shepherd their flocks to the beach so that everybody can be together.

As for recreation in general throughout the year, its enjoyment is, of course, enhanced when it is shared, but that doesn't mean that the husband's and wife's recreational interest need always be identical. One does not have to participate in one's husband's or wife's outside interests to share and enjoy them. A young woman who played golf with her fiancé all through their courtship and engagement period, seldom played with him after marriage. Because his professional associates through the week were women, she felt he needed the companionship of men in his "off" hours. For her part she joined a sketching class and as she phrased it, "took her golf sitting down." Two outside interests introduced into a family are better than one, if there is a sympathetic sharing and not mere tolerrance. Contacts with other persons in a recreational capacity now and then bring later returns to one's own family. Variety is essential not only for recreational benefit but for the renewal and vitality of interest in each other.

One kind of recreation which is less an activity than a personal asset is interest in the arts—music, literature, drama, the fine arts of painting, sculpture, architecture. Similarities in these cultural interests are much more important than in the purely active kinds of recreation such as skating or swimming, for example. They serve as an intrinsic part of the whole personality, develop kindred thoughts and yield dividends over and over. When two persons live together as man and wife, year after year, the differences lessen and the likenesses increase. They have accepted each other and because they have, there develops a gradual oneness of mind and heart. Yet, the oneness need not destroy the quality that gives marriage its vitality, for that lies in the ever-constant inspiration two wedded personalities find in each other, which, while it gives, also receives.

Chapter VII

Finances and the Working Wife

MONEY! Those hard, unromantic dollars which nevertheless give our marriage its opportunity and then often, before we realize it, bring it to an end, or, at least, rob it of its peace and happiness.

Financial difficulties are not Enemy No. 1 to marriage happiness. Rarely is divorce attributable to money itself. Neither women nor men value it to that extent. It is the way money is managed, the way the power is used, that causes the trouble. To a man, his bank account is the measure of his success. To a woman, it is the measure of her independence. As a wife, whether she earns the money or not is not so important as her right to whatever is there, her free unquestioned accessibility to it. Marriage gives her that right. With all his worldly goods he has her endowed.

Not too long ago for some of us to remember, most women were perfectly content to be supported by their husbands, never thought to question their dependence, even though a vanguard of "Woman's Righters" were striving to waken them. Income-making and provision for their families were solely the responsibility of husbands. Homemaking and taking care of its members were the responsibility of wives. These divisions of labor were as fixed as the stars— barring war, flood, and fire.

When a thoughtful young bridegroom of that era handed his bride her first housekeeping money with a smile that said, "You won't have to ask for it this time, at least," she didn't quite understand. What was there to be hesitant about? She would have asked for it, even this first time, as nonchalantly as she would have asked for the house key if she had needed it. She was the mistress of his home—empty purse, empty larder. There was no "mine and thine." There couldn't be. Yet, increasingly today, there is. There are two heads to the household, two sources of supply, two minds to govern. If only they do not choose two conflicting pathways with divergent goals! And they need not. What is more, they increasingly do not, as they come under the influence of higher education and a greater knowledge of themselves and their contributing capacities.

Compulsory attendance at school into the upper grades, advanced degrees for thousands more have produced a type of man and woman who are conditioned to work side by side in domestic life as they worked side by side in school life. When under stress of labor shortage caused by military service, women slipped in to fill men's places, that, too, was understood. What perhaps took everyone unawares was the amazing aptitude of woman in industry, and the independence it created for her. She had moved up, she knew. Henceforth she could take care of herself, and, increasingly, she does.

But she can also do a lot of other things with her new earning capacity. She can provide for her future, facilitate her own marriage, if single, or, if married, help her husband through a tight spot in his business, or send him to graduate school to get his doctorate, or register for a refresher course, or she can take out hospitalization insurance or save for the children's college expenses. What can't they do and don't they do, these women, with their new-found economic resources!

The comforting thing about it to the men is that there are so many employed wives floating about wherever you go—about six million of them—that they don't have to be worried any more about their own prestige as breadwinners. "My husband didn't take at all to the idea of my working," one wife quoted in a chatty noon hour. "What does that make me look like?" he asked.

"Ha! My job was my husband's idea in the first place. He thought I ought to get away from home more. I think now he likes the shirts I get him at cost!"

This husband was right. The average, well-educated American woman needs her domesticity diluted.

Her kitchen is more attractive than it was in the past, now a cross between a tearoom with its ruffled curtains and a laboratory with its buzzing appliances. But her part in it is less creative. She goes through the motions indicated on the bright fancy labels of various ready-mixes but she has no more than squared off before she is through, with money back if she is not a success —a success at reading and following directions. "Born cooks," you must know, have gone for keeps.

These women, whose kitchens have so recently been mechanized, love their homes, their husbands, and their children, but they need challenging occupations and need them beyond their own doorsteps. They need to be part of a group, a productive group—sales force, staff, faculty, or executive board. They need to feel themselves identified with the interests that the magazines present to them—political, economic, educational. Acceptable, even necessary as her earnings may be to herself and family, the greater gain to the married woman from outside employment comes to the woman herself. It pulls her together, strengthens her ego, broadens her outlook, gives her a chance to go as far as she feels she can go and that, in this twentieth century, is pretty far, for the world has need of leadership and supporters of leaders as never before.

Yet, with all the woman's growth and expansion, economically and personally, the practical working out of details between husband and wife in their home has brought many heartaches, sometimes warfare and even disunion. For smooth operation, the implications of a wife's earning power must be recognized before marriage and reckoned with even though she does no active earning after marriage. Potentially or actually, she presents a special challenge to her husband, the first part of which is financial.

INITIAL COST

"How much does it take to get married, anyway?" every young man questions, directly after he has found his girl.

"Two dollars at the license bureau," his buddy will reply, and that is just about the only definite answer he will ever get. The amount of ready money needed to marry and set up housekeeping depends upon circumstances and living standards. Yet young people today are so thoroughly independent and self-sufficient, they approach their marriages as they approach their studies or their college degrees, with readiness to make all kinds of sacrifices. "We have two kitchen chairs," a theological student said recently, "a table, a desk, and a bed." Others, who have left school and are earning comfortable salaries, are more affluent with their pay checks and credit rating which bring shining refrigerators and television sets installment-wise to their doors.

Traditionally, of course, men bargained for their wives with herds of cattle, acres of land, storehouses of grain. But today whether for better or for worse, marriage has become, so far as tangible assets are concerned, a pretty empty-handed affair. Brides do not even bring to it the hope chests of their grandmothers' time, packed with fine linens and silver. Instead, both men and women bring their education, their college degrees and technical skills, their jobs and social securities. With good school records, good junior work cards, and a job with a promising future sewed up, few young couples hesitate to marry even if no bank balance stands behind them. "I am my bank balance!" a young fellow said confidently the other day. And barring the unforeseen, he is!

Either way, with available money or without it, the need during the first married years is not for an equipped and well-furnished house. Change is the order of the day—change in location, in business opportunity, in the size of the growing family, in personal affairs. All of these make the casually furnished, temporary home the logical choice. The pleasure comes not in the buying of new furnishings but in the creation of one's own—a few visits to a used furniture place or an auction sale, an "ad" or two in the Sunday paper, a semester at evening school learning about furniture repair and upholstery, and there you are, with everything that you need and the fun of making it besides! A home to be a home must grow in form and feeling as its makers grow, little by little, day by day.

The energies of old-time housewives were spent in maintaining their families—cooking, sewing, mending, preserving, and canning. The energies of today's housewives are, or can be, spent in creating a home, a do-it-yourself home, in every spot inside and out, that can elude the gadget-makers both great and small. So much for the start, the "one for the money": a little ready cash for the pushoff, an intelligent weighing of all factors to keep reality and dreams in balance, and a spirit of the creative running in high gear to make all possible.

SHARING THE LOAD

Yes, marriage goes ahead today on a shoestring basis with little doubt that the double income has much to do in making it attainable. It is the thing young people do today. Yet for the sake of romance few girls like to feel that their contribution is taken for granted and deep down in their hearts they would like to be the first to volunteer their aid. "Look, Man, I'm here, don't forget me and my little old job. It's good for as long as we need it." They would also like to know when their husbands will take over and permit them to become housekeepers and mothers, before too late, "before," as one girl put it, "I expect a baby's bed to be as dry as a filing cabinet."

Occasionally, one meets or hears of a home-brew sort of girl who does not care to work at all. To her, marriage is not marriage, wifedom is not wifedom, if she must continue to follow the same route each day to office, to schoolroom, to shop, back and forth the same old shuttle as before. No, not the same, for her pay check, she feels, would be lost in the welter of household necessities.

When such a girl rejects her sweetheart on the basis of "insufficient funds," breaks her engagement after a mutual avowal of love, a man wonders—was he asking too much of love, or wasn't there any in the first place, or was there only love of what money could buy rather than of what money could do?

It is not usually love of money so much at it is lack of vision, imagination, and, yes, faith that stops them. As one such girl explained, "It hurt to give Ted up, but I was afraid that once I had begun, I could just keep on forever. You never know."

Yet every girl has ample opportunity to know whether her fiancé will be a good provider. She may not know his potentials when she first falls in love with him, but they do not remain obscure very long. If he is a student working toward a college degree, the application he gives to his studies, his rank in his class, the honors and citations he has won all tell the story.

Or, if he is a young fellow starting out in business, the history of his employment, his promotions and salary raises give authentic assurance of a secure future—as secure as human destiny ever is.

Rarely need a girl feel that once she has contributed her earnings she will always have to. Most men are happy to have home-staying wives and cradles filled with babies. Women who continue their outside employment after the husband's income is adequate for both usually do so for personal reasons, from choice. They like the luxury afforded by combined resources, or, successful and happy in their employment, they hesitate to relinquish it, partly from fear of not duplicating it later and partly from fear of boredom. "What does one do all day around home?" one business girl asked. Somebody answer her!

Yet, whether a girl retires to become a "lady of leisure" or to have her family, the time comes when she longs to return to the adventure and challenge that comes from making her contribution to the world of work. As one well-to-do, generously supported wife expressed it when she applied for a somewhat mediocre position, "My pocketbook doesn't need this money, but my soul, my ego does. I feel like a parasite when I have nothing to show for my keep."

The Personal Relationship

One of the hazards of the marriage that maps out too long a pull for the wife who is to be chief bread-winner while her husband earns his higher degree in, say, law, medicine, or engineering, is the change in the personal relationship. With both husband and wife dedicated to the one mighty effort of future accomplishment, the needs of the present are frequently lost sight of. There is little if any leisure. When the wife is not down at the office earning the family income, she is at home getting meals and probably transcribing research data and notes for a student husband. "Hands in the dishpan, fingers on the keys," one wife chanted merrily as she hurried from kitchen to study and back again on her "off hours." Sleep for both is always scanty and restless, there is little recreation, little social life, no money for suitable dressing even if there were any, or for reciprocal invitations. Husband and wife strip themselves down to the less-than-human level of diversion, all in anticipation of the future. There is no today. Even the sex life has gradually faded away in the atmosphere of austere living. Study, study . . . cram, cram . . . write, write . . . type, type.

When all is done, when after four or five years the grind is over and the M.D.'s or Ph.D.'s are trailing after the husband's name and they seek each other in joy and gratitude, all may not be as it once was. Love, for the moment at least, has fled, and they are again strangers. That mysterious, inexplicable something has occurred which unfortunately now and then does occur when love is too long sacrificed to outward circumstances, or has been transmuted into an alien energy, slow to return. Tragically, each is still capable of response to another one unassociated with the denial. But loyalty usually forbids desertion in thought or deed and the outer bond, empty-hearted, holds.

A variation of this student-wife estrangement often repeats itself in a business situation when husband and wife have pooled resources in money, energy, and time to become business partners. Such a couple, if I interpret them correctly, have been passing my door by the clock for several years. When I first observed them they were a bent and somber pair who walked silently and apart, one slightly behind the other. Today, their joint effort, whatever it is, is prospering. The two are dressing better. They are wearing lighter, brighter colors, and walking closer together, abreast of each other, and there is a bond of intimacy between them. For years I did not know the relationship and thought they might be brother and sister, but now I know they are not. And I know something more. I know that husband and wife can give all to one mighty external objective and still have something left for each other. "For what," if we may paraphrase St. Mark, "is a man profited if he gain the whole world and lose his own wife?"

CHECKING ACCOUNTS AND BANKING

practical —

When the pinch-penny days are over and there is enough money to begin thinking about checking and savings accounts, many decisions are in order. Shall just one joint account be opened, to be drawn upon by both husband and wife, or shall there be two accounts, with separate deposits? Here is something to think about, for there is more to this matter of banking than meets the eye, more than meets the ear, more than the hearsay of friend or neighbor who offers ready advice.

Opening a checking account is not just putting some money in the bank and drawing it out again. It is not just the modern equivalent of storing away a few dollars in an old sugar bowl on the pantry shelf. A checking account is a valid, personal, financial endorsement. You use it to open charge accounts, to borrow money, to buy travelers' checks, to carry on your business. Man or woman, husband or wife, everyone needs the prestige and security a bank account affords—and bank accounts cost money!

Banks *today* are not too arbitrary about standing balances, but the number of checks permitted to be drawn without charge depends upon the size of the balance. The larger the base deposit, or standing balance, the greater the number of checks permitted without service charge. Familywise, a joint account gives each one, husband and wife, a better idea of "where the money goes" and holds down some of those tempting little (or big) extravagances otherwise likely to creep in and bring about deficits, to say nothing of raising personal questions—"George, dear, I thought we weren't going to . . ."

Wives of an older generation rarely shared a joint account or had one of their own. One wife reveals that she made out her first deposit slip and wrote her first check as her very-ill husband signed his last—a tragic ceremony many times repeated in the not too distant years just past. A few women today, even including those who earn their own money, still bank indirectly through their husbands—many, but not all, as a matter of convenience. "Tom's the banker in this house. Figures and I tangle too easily."

A lawyer whose special field is the settling of estates and probating of wills says that most of his women clients know very little about money in general, and less of their husband's individual holdings. Occasionally a man's estate falls far below expectations, judged by his standard of living, but usually it reveals much more. Whichever it is, and whether the wife has enjoyed luxuries she should not have had, or has been deprived of necessities she should have had, she cries out from the depths of her belated awareness, "Why didn't he let me know!"

We wonder, too, why do so many men leave their wives in a financial fog when complete understanding is to everyone's advantage? Increasingly, as women demonstrate their ability to make money, they are feeling the need of knowing how to handle it and recognize that an account in their own name is the first step in that direction. Yet husbands are not always responsive to the idea. "Why does she want a separate account? She gets all she wants, doesn't she? I'm not holding out on her, am I?"

What she wants is difficult for many husbands to understand. She wants recognition in her own right. She, herself, Margaret Billings Smith (or whatever), wants the personal independence and dignity that her signature on a check will give her. Also, as the person in charge of a household, she wants to be able to meet any need or emergency when it arises and not be left without resources because her husband has overdrawn or failed to deposit his pay check promptly. More than that, an account of her own will put an end to those wifely little subterfuges which all women know and many are driven to adopt when legitimate family funds are not available—the increasing demands for an unjustified larger housekeeping budget in order to permit a backlog of personal savings; the returning of merchandise for credit bought for cash, to meet an extra need; the borrowing of supplies from friends and neighbors; and even, at times, in desperation, the playing of the races or a few rounds of bridge just to provide herself with a bit of needed money not in the budget—all of these just to "avoid asking." "Ask, ask, ask! Why do I have to ask? Isn't it mine, as well as his?" Yes, it is hers, and her husband would be the first to admit it. "My dear, it is all yours!" But he still likes his bank account under his own name, alone.

Today, when much of the world's wealth is in the possession of women, either through inheritance or through their own efforts, their first obligation to those who have labored to earn it, whether themselves or others, is the gaining of a sound knowledge of money's management. The earning and protective power of property in this money-abundant country through investments of numberless kinds—savings deposits, securities, insurance benefits, stocks and bonds and the rest—should be passed on to a wife in theory as well as in practice. If women are going to become the custodians of the country's wealth as well as the makers and dispensers of it, they must be given the day-by-day education and training in the actual science of business administration—buying, selling, investing, saving—no matter how small the first beginnings. Who would gain more from this tutelage than a husband himself during his lifetime? But would he be the best tutor? Perhaps not. Better the impersonal, trained instructor in an organized class, or a private tutor. A little book with a disturbing title, *Teach Your Wife To Be a Widow*, by Donald I. Rodgers, is of enormous value.

Although wives will learn more readily from trained instructors, fathers can be good teachers of their sons and daughters, and introduce them into the science of banking and accounting when the first allowances are worked out together. It is the boy or girl who has had training and experience in the earning and use of money who will make a responsible breadwinner as well as a good custodian and heir of the family's fortunes when in later years it falls to him.

DIVISION OF EARNINGS

Banking is one thing. Division of income, allocation of amounts especially as they concern the expenditures for the household and personal needs, is another. Who pays for what and how much?

A husband, let us say, earns $5,000 a year against his wife's $2,500. Five thousand is a living wage and a man likes to feel he's supporting his family. "If she wants more than I make," one husband said, "she can provide it herself. But I buy the groceries!" Another husband recognized that the overhead expenses of a household increase considerably when the wife and housekeeper is absent. "It is just good business," he said, "to deduct all extra expenses before you declare a net gain."

Much has been said both humorously and seriously about "what profit the working wife?" Aside from a more extensive wardrobe than stay-at-homes require, there is often the second automobile and its upkeep, lunches five days a week, and frequently dinners. "Jack, the cupboard is as bare as a bone. Let's stay downtown tonight," to say nothing of the stitch-in-time on everybody's clothes which is so hard to manage when nobody is at home to stitch. Extra expenses creep up consumingly, and the net gain in the end is like the disappearing core of the little boy's apple.

Yet, for all this, there is a long-range gain when experience has brought about a systematized way of lessening the drain, and salary increases have created a margin large enough to overshadow expenses. When this happens, "going to work" will not be such a discouraging business to many women and a most valuable lesson in the fundamental principles of finance will have been learned—specifically, the difference between net and gross incomes, often a difficult concept for the feminine mind.

Although studies and surveys assure us that the employment of a wife does not increase marriage hazards, in the end (if there are no children) it often does affect the quality of the home life and in occasional instances acts as an alienating factor. A woman who has developed far enough in her work to feel the pull of it as one does in the professions—the arts and sciences, for example, and yes, in the executive levels of business—may be caught in a new kind of love triangle. Her hours at home are unshared hours (we don't talk shop!), her musings, unshared musings (I get new ideas when I am doing my housework at night). Unless she is one of those wives who are able to dismiss their business interests and ideas and become all wife during home hours, protests may arise. "Does that piece of work *have* to be done this evening?"

One of the prices a woman and her husband sometimes pay for their skill and contribution to the economic scene is the lessening of their activities in the community and the curtailment of their homes as social centers. Men like their womenfolk to be socially minded and equipped. They like to invite a visiting bigwig to dinner on short notice, or to ask the office "gang" in for cocktails now and then. They like to belong to a local club or two and see their names in the evening paper. But who, except the very few, can afford the luxury of a $200 (or more) a month housekeeper to have everything all scrubbed and polished and the wheels moving when they return at night? Fatigue, expense, restricted social and community life are the price the employed woman pays for her service to the larger work of the world.

Yet it is this desiring to be somebody, to extend one-self, to break the routine and isolation of work that starts trouble. "I don't mind company and a little fun, but I don't like Jim's crowd," one wife explained. "They pile in here by the dozens on a Friday or Saturday night and drink up all the money we've both saved for a month." Or perhaps it is the husband who deplores his wife's conviviality. "We go out to dinner for a little celebration of our own. Not content, she picks up another couple, then it's a quick stop at the liquor store, and where are we? Out of pocket for another week." Others differ on home expenses. "Dick wants to let the world know he's had a raise—so it's a swimming pool in the back yard and a new Buick at the curb." "I hate raises!" another wife cried tearfully. "For every dollar increase we go two in the hole."

Or a husband exclaims, "Why does she have to have a fur coat when every inch of pipe in the plumbing system needs ripping out?" When two persons, man and wife, really care, they strive to meet the needs and cravings of each other in any or every direction, social or otherwise, and adjust their differences. But when quarrels and disagreements such as these are constantly coming up, either between employed or unemployed wives and their husbands, something is wrong with the whole relationship, and it isn't money! Money and the spending of money are merely the ten-pins set up at the end of the alley for each to knock down. Wife knocks down husband's pins, husband knocks down wife's. It is a sorry business. No plan of budgeting or allocating of funds will take care of these people. The correction must come through a removal of the cause of the difficulty—whether it lies in the personal relationship of the two partners, or in some existing premarriage conflict within one or the other which would motivate his (or her) spending wherever he was or whomever he had married. Money is power. It is an instrument which people in distress unwittingly call upon to further their needs of whatever nature, just as others call upon sex.

A husband who felt that his wife had become indifferent to him, consciously or unconsciously, punished her by bringing home a succession of pedigreed cats, Siamese or angora, to which she was allergic. "How can he! He knows I can't endure them!" his agonized wife would cry. "But that was long ago," her husband would temporize, "and *I* like them!"

Differences that arise not out of the present but out of the past often break forth in frugality or extravagance in spending. The wife of a minor executive who was just coming up through the ranks after a long struggle had always bought her hats, in the lean days, at the church bazaars. "But, my dear," her husband protested, "you know you don't have to, any more." Besides, hadn't he noticed his chief's wife wearing a similar hat not long ago? "Two years ago," his wife replied, "but nobody remembers hats and this one is as good as new for a dollar and a half!"

Thrift, with many, is a religion. It is built in. You can't teach them to discard anything, not even thrift. Extravagance is something different. It is a disease, an illness, and can more readily be taken care of. Usually it springs from a sense of personal inadequacy, or deprivation which must compensate for a hardship of some sort—lack of love, success, home care, confidence, or other essential to the inner personal self or psyche. Building up the ego, helping the extravagant person to achieve in his own right, will increase his feelings of accomplishment. As in alcoholism, when the wine of the spirit runs rich and full, the wine in the flask will run dry.

The economically productive wife and the double income her activities create have come to stay. The Br'er Rabbit concept of the sacrificed husband, "I goes up as you goes down; you'll get to the bottom all safe and soun'" which one hears on every hand, is but the usual and to-be-expected protest against social change. Authority is easy, cooperation is not; but if it is pursued jointly it yields the riches and satisfactions that come from the stimulation of two active personalities working toward a common goal. When, that is, all is well with the heart, finances will not be a disuniting factor.

There is an old saying "When poverty comes in the

door, love flies out the window." When money comes in the door, one must watch the windows. Money can readily become both a promoter and a disrupter of home and family ties. Which it is depends upon the strength of the bond between the two who make the home.

Chapter VIII

Storks on the Rooftree

SOONER or later the stork flies over the homes of most young married couples and makes its welcome nest in the chimney pots of most of them. It is then that all wives, employed as well as unemployed, meet on the common ground of woman's supreme vocation, childbearing. It is then, too, that their husbands, for the time being at least, stand by in a kind of detached wonderment. "Could I really have done this?" Or, are they invaded by an unexpected envy such as must come to many a husband whose wife has been appointed to a diplomatic post or who ascends a judicial bench or is elected to some other prominent position?

Yet, husbands are rapidly becoming identified with the experience of pregnancy and childbirth, and liking it. They are discovering that the advent of parenthood today, in all its phases, is far from being the catch-as-catch-can affair that it has been for generations in our country when the pitching was left in the hands of the gods and baby-making and baby care were matters of tradition.

The substitute for chance and the methods of other days is the modern twin science of gynecology and obstetrics, with their psychiatric overtones of emo-

121

tional as well as physical fitness for parenthood. When this twofold readiness comes to flower in the marriage bond, it is felt as a warm and eager expectancy which, in the end, not only furthers conception, but fosters the immediate environment of the developing embryo itself. We are all just beginning to realize how much a state of mind has to contribute to a woman's fertility.

Organized sources for the direction and guidance of young prospective parents are available everywhere with and without expense—Red Cross classes, Planned Parenthood Centers, church groups, nursery schools, even municipal courts have clinics for expectant fathers and mothers in mixed and separate classes. Their questions indicate the trend of their interest. They ask about:

1. The best number of children to have, and when to have them;
2. The cost of each baby—(cheaper by the dozen?);
3. The possibility of influencing of a baby's sex;
4. The modern treatment of sterility;
5. The effectiveness of contraception;
6. The technique of artificial insemination.

All these and other questions are answered with the latest findings that today's experience and research have yielded. In addition, book and magazine editors, alert to the rapidly growing interest on the part of young parents and the public, are seeking to supply the best, most authoritative knowledge available to meet the understanding of everyone: the man and woman in the street, the wife in her home, the student in the classroom. With the birth rate increasingly higher, the parents younger (many in their teens), the yardstick of even the recent generations is no longer reliable in terms of scholastic findings. What is there for young husbands and wives but to make a business of marriage and prepare for it professionally? Show me a pregnant young woman today who would allow herself to gain weight without limit; live in seclusion for nine months from a sense of modesty, or listen to music to produce a musician in her child. There simply aren't any.

To start with the first question in the above list—The best number of children to have, and when to have them.

The answer—how can one answer? There are too many factors to be considered. Health, wealth, circumstances could change an opinion even if it were wise to offer one. Most young people are influenced by the number of children they grew up with. "I had three in my family. I'd like three." Or the opposite, "I was an only child; I'll never ask a child of mine to grow up alone." In spite of the trend of women to become wage-earners, when it comes to children today, they want a large family. "I am looking forward to four." Until very recently two was the average. They wanted just a boy and a girl.

You ask, how soon after marriage?

For answer, another "It depends." Generally speaking, because there are so many situations to meet, setting up housekeeping, two persons learning to adapt to each other's personal ways and to family ways, and becoming a new sex partner, the first year of marriage is no time to invite a baby into the scene of action.

The second year?

Probably, if all concerned are quickly adaptable people and the budget is adequate. A baby is a plant, a tiny, sensitive, living organism. He is dependent upon his environment for growth. He must be given warmth, sunshine, and required substances for his very existence, both of body and of spirit. If his home yields anxiety, conflict, distrust, misunderstandings that chill and impoverish his environment, the baby becomes restless, sluggish, and retarded in both his physical and emotional growth. The unforseeable effects are not always recognized. "He's just that kind of baby," one hears parents explain. But the chances are he is not. He has been made that kind of baby through the life about him.

Fancifully speaking, I should like to give to every baby the same right to voluntary existence (choice of birth) that we are permitting his mother and father in regard to voluntary parenthood. How often one has heard a child say resentfully in after years, "I didn't ask to be born"? No, he didn't, and parents have the unending obligation not to cause him to regret that he was!

The following are a few questionable reasons which would suggest that the time was not opportune for a baby's birth from the standpoint of his welfare, however much the parents themselves, one or both, might be benefited.

1. A period when parents are drifting apart.
   "Children draw people together."
2. Socially timid parents who need "ice-breakers."
   "Everyone is attracted to children."
3. Wives who need companionship.
   "My wife gets lonesome when I'm away."
4. Parents who experiment in search of a preferred sex.
   "We wanted a boy, but we got three girls first" or,
   "We wanted a girl, but we got three boys first."
5. Parents who plan to exploit their children.
   "My family are troupers. We want young blood in it to keep the name going."

The best and only motive for starting a family of children, and fortunately more people claim this motive, is the natural spontaneous desire to have them. Most husbands and wives feel a need to round out and enrich their marriage in the close relationship of the parent job. They like to feel too that they are leaving something of themselves in the world of which they have been a part.

Because a baby may not choose his parents or his time to be born we must make the choice for him, be his deputies, choose the time, be the parents any baby would wish. A large order, but one that is becoming a world-wide custom—more and better homes for more and better babies.

PREGNANCY

In spite of hope deferred for a year or two, young couples are vitally concerned with all the aspects of pregnancy, its identification, its stages of development, the mother's weight and diet control, and finally the termination—the hospital experience and care, anaesthetics and the rest.

Psychologically, pregnancy is always taking place in the mind of some young wives, even though they have chosen postponement in the interest of everyone. Theirs is a kind of dream pregnancy like that of some infertile women. "But you wouldn't want it all out of your hands," a friend said to one of these waiting girls, "and just take what comes when it comes as our grandmothers used to do." "I would and I wouldn't," she answered. She would, because she didn't like to wait. She wouldn't, because she wouldn't want to miss that exciting dramatic moment when the two of them, she and her Bob or Bill, would prayerfully, reverently consecrate their marriage to the creation of their first child.

Almost everyone knows the symptoms of pregnancy, but because many "false alarms" occur with both new and experienced mothers, doctors remind us that there are two series of evidences, the probable and the sure. The probable, to most of us, are traditionally sudden sensitiveness of the breasts, circulatory changes bringing dizziness and faintness, morning nausea, and, most familiar of all, absence of the menstrual period. Yet, all of these indications including the "missed" period may, at times, be due to other causes. On the other hand, pregnancy may be established with menstruation still present at the usual time, but in decreasing strength, or it may even occur before there ever has been a menstrual period, as in the case of the child bride in the Orient where marriage was consummated before maturing. Fairly frequent in our country is the beginning of a new pregnancy, unexpected because of breast feeding, before menstruation has returned from the last baby's birth.

The unfailing sure diagnosis of pregnancy can be made about the fifth month when first movements or quickening can be felt in gentle fluttering or thrusts against the mother's side, a corresponding rapid little heartbeat, heard through the doctor's stethoscope, and an X-ray picture that catches the baby's outline removes all doubt. Yet five months is a long time to wait for some parents to know positively and legal decisions often depend upon exact date of conception. Today many tests have been worked out which are able to establish the presence or absence of pregnancy in three to four weeks after exposure, and to give the report in a few hours. If the patient is pregnant a specimen of her urine injected into a female laboratory rabbit will show positive evidence of reproductive activity in her ovaries. If she isn't, the little rabbit, of course, is unaffected.

The Obstetrician

The very best promotional work any obstetrician can have comes through the mothers whose babies "he has brought into the world." Over the teacups, or, to speak more modernly, during the coffe hour, much talk about hospitals, doctors, methods of childbirth, natural or traditional, different kinds of anaesthetics, and so on, drift about among young marrieds who gather up a lot of information against the day when they shall need a doctor to see them through.

Yet in the end, there is but one choice, the man himself. You chose your physician; hospital and method go along with him. He has his pets in analgesics and drugs. You don't question. But the selection of this man or woman who will have your destiny and that of your child in his keeping, that is your choice, and that is vital. It may mean the difference between having your baby or not having him in all his rightful perfection.

The man you want holds his position because he has earned it by never failing to win and hold a patient's confidence. She knows he will see her through and bring her baby through as carefully as though he were the last child on earth and all future mankind depended on his life, like Noah in his ark. Confidence in one's obstetrician means not only confidence in the outcome, but because of the assurance he inspires, and the fears that depart, also the ability to make a greater contribution to the baby's triumphal delivery.

The modern human being is not a heroic person so far as enduring pain is concerned. And as American women we like to be intelligent about the sort of relief our chosen physician uses and why. Analgesics and anaesthetics are the team of drugs most commonly used to ease the pain of childbirth. The analgesics are used in the first part of labor to bring about a state of mind (amnesia) which dims or blots out memory so that the pain, though felt, is not recalled. "Nothing to it," a young mother will say. "I didn't feel a thing!" The anaesthetics which are used in the last stages of labor bring about semi or total unconsciousness. "I went to sleep and when I woke up it was all over! I was back in my bed nice as you please."

The advantages of these two drugs used in combination is not so much to relieve pain as to give the doctor, the baby, and his mother a chance to work together to a successful delivery that assures an injury-free baby and mother. Haste and the consequence of haste, lack of precision, are far more destructive than the use of analgesics and anaesthetics in competent hands.

CHILDBIRTH PATTERNS

Time was when, without benefit of any relieving drugs, women lay down "when their time had come," bore the pain, and delivered their babies on their own. We wonder how! Today pain-reducing or pain-relieving drugs are here, but they are not the whole story. In our time a whole galaxy of methods of administering them has been worked out, not only to eliminate labor pains, but to eliminate fear and give maximum benefits to both mother and child. All of them have had considerable vogue and have been adopted enthusiastically by both physician and patient. Twilight Sleep was the first of the new childbirth patterns, and bears a name which in itself made strong appeal. It produced a semi-conscious condition in which the patient was aware of sensation but had no memory of it later. The spinal anaesthesias have no such beguiling name, but they are very popular because their pain-reducing effects carry through into the last difficult stage of labor.

But the triumph of the century in the minds of many is the method called natural childbirth, not because it has done away with pain-relieving drugs, but because it has brought about a frame of mind free from panic, and inspired women with pride and joy in childbearing. Through exercises, diet, recreation, and rhythmical group activities during pregnancy they have come to feel themselves not victims but victors as they face their confinement. Physically strengthened and relaxed they are emotionally prepared by a philosophy which looks upon childbirth as an achievement. How much this state of mind means to the attending physician all of us can imagine!

HOME OR HOSPITAL

Many of us who have taken ourselves off to a hospital for the births of our babies do not realize how many women there are who elect to remain at home. They like the comfort of their families and like to keep a motherly and domestic eye upon their households.

"But it is so much safer at a hospital," someone will say. Not safer if one has a skilled doctor, but better in case of an emergency, for a modern, well-equipped maternity ward has every mechanized aid—inhalators, exhalators, incubators—ready at hand and in addition there are the parents' training classes which help make confident and easy transition between hospital and home care, an enormous benefit to baby as well as to parents.

Perhaps these home-delivered mothers are responsible for the introduction of one of the later types of hospital service, "rooming in," which closely approximates the home situation. The plan allows a mother to have her baby direct from the delivery room where, in its little transparent plastic bed which can swing over her bed and with a cabinet of bathing and toilet equipment close at hand, she may take over the care of her baby just as she would in her own nursery at home. This having one's brand-new child whisked away into a village of baby beds all in a row like cottages on a street, with not a glimpse of him except at feeding time, has never made strong appeal to new mothers after a long nine-month stretch of blind waiting.

And what the "rooming-in" plan must do for the baby himself; feeling the gentle, unhurried touch of mother's hands and the sound of her soft voice in contrast to the compounded wailing of a regiment of baby cries in the hospital nursery. That is beyond words to express.

THE COST OF BABIES

Babies cost money. One must not leave the subject of early decisions—doctors, hospitals, rooming-in, deliveries—without a word concerning expenses. Though it is heavy for some young couples, there are ways of meeting it: baby-saving plans, like Christmas-saving plans, for one. You put in your bit regularly every week, enough to count, but not too much to spare lest you forsake your purpose and discourage the family. Just to try it out there are plain toy banks at home, locked tight against raiding. In no time at all it can collect enough, as the prospective father may say, shaking it, to pay for one-sixth of a baby, or one-fourth or one-half—eventually a whole.

Communities differ in their scale of prices, but the average cost for first-class service would probably be close to $400 or $500. It depends. The obstetrician might ask $200 or more, including prenatal and postnatal care for the first year, to be paid by arrangement. Hospitals, generally speaking, ask about $120 to $135 with payments in advance, depending on, of course, whether a private or a shared room is desired. The accessories of the anaesthetics and other services, incubator if it should be needed, will take another few dollars.

The husband's hospital insurance plan often carries a maternity clause for a wife, say $50 to $100 for each baby. But whether a mother decides to take advantage of this very moderate sum or to retain a private obstetrician would depend to considerable extent upon her individual situation, both physically and financially. An insurance medical service is usually worked out on a group basis and has both advantages and disadvantages. If the group of physicians is small, limited to three or four, each of whom has seen the patient during her pregnancy and followed her progress, the plan works out very well, but if she faces a stranger every time she has a check-up, or at her delivery, the plan is questionable. She loses confidence. A private physician establishes a personal relationship. He knows her not only as Mrs. Williams, due late in March, but he knows, as no one else can know, every nook and cranny of her constantly changing insides. However, some insurance companies are becoming very flexible in the management of their maternity services, and are allowing mothers to remain with their own private physicians, depending upon the nature of their policy.

Women who have experienced difficulty in their pregnancies or in coming to full term or from prolonged labor with an earlier child would hesitate before setting aside a personal physician to deliver her. His skillful week-by-week direction of the pregnancy is essential. Moreover, if he is the true physician that he should be, he will be no Shylock in his financial demands.

The Waiting Period

That nine-month stretch which many women dread —"you look so!"—isn't a waiting period at all until the last few weeks, and looks have been so greatly redeemed through the professional touch by maternity dress specialists that one looks very sporty and modern—only a little different in one's gay smocks—from one's husband in his tails-outside, Hawaiian shirts. There is no time in a pregnancy period today for idle waiting. It is jampacked with activities—the doctor's schedule plus ordinary domestic routine, plus getting the baby's layette and nursery in readiness, and if one is enterprising, the formation of or attendance at a Stork Club.

These clubs, which started a generation ago, have grown in number and purpose. Originally they were purely social affairs—with baby showers for each member somewhere along the line. But the modern young woman is not only socially but educationally minded. Her luncheons and showers are likely to be interspersed or supplemented with book reviews and discussions on baby care and family life topics.

Not so formally organized, but much older in practice is the Nursery Exchange, which acts as a clearing-house and passes along outgrown and used articles of baby equipment—baths, toilet chairs, high chairs, beds, blankets, cradles, all sorts of things including baby wardrobe items. The saving is unbelievable, and sometimes a special article becomes so popular it is spoken for months in advance. One mother boasts that the cradle of her firstborn (now old enough to have his own baby) has been in almost constant use among her friends for a generation. Had its future been foreseen, no doubt each successive little occupant would have left his name plate on it, with date affixed to enrich its heritage.

When at last the great day arrives, announced by intermittent pains and twinges, with mother's handbag long-since packed, and father's gas tank filled to the brim, the doctor is first to be notified. "Plenty of time, plenty of time," he may say cheerfully. "Call me again when the pains become more frequent and stronger." Or, he may have explained in advance: Labor is divided into three stages. The first and longest brings about the contractions of the muscles of the uterine walls which press upon the baby in his bag of water and start him on his way. His compressible little head and the water sac act as a uniting wedge to bring about the stretching of the cervix, that tight narrow passage which leads into the vagina or birth canal, and is capable of stretching sufficiently to permit the passage of considerable bulk of baby, seven, eight, nine or more pounds of him. The doctor may have explained all this in brief; first labor pains are not severe, occur at intervals with rest spaces between, which become increasingly shorter as pains become stronger. When the water sac bursts, as it does normally under the continued pressure, the first step of labor should be close to accomplishment in the distension of the cervix. But sometimes the fluid drains away even before labor begins and prolongs the first period of stretching.

An old-time horse and buggy doctor tells how he used to keep up the courage of his patients during the long pull of opening up a resisting cervix by haranguing them in the fashion of a county fair auctioneer. "A dime, a dime! Come, come, can't you give me something bigger than a dime?" Then, after a few minutes of rest, "A nickel, a nickel! That's better, I thought you could. How about a quarter? I need at least a quarter this time. That's the girl! Now, how about a half dollar? Not so bad, let's make it a whole round dollar!" So, he coaxed and inspired and worked with his patient. It was tough going—none of the new modern methods of relief were available—but there were rest periods between and at last when the opening was "as large as two dollars" a whiff of chloroform brought sleep and oblivion.

The second stage of labor, short and severe, is today usually accomplished under some form of anaesthesia, semi or complete. With each strong contraction the patient gets a renewal "shot" or whiff or whatnot to help her through, and at the final moment of expulsion, an added amount which usually blots her out completely, though it sometimes leaves her with a waking consciousness, enough, if she is lucky, to see her blessed child lifted out into the light of day.

The third stage of labor finishes up the job. The remaining membranes, if there are any fragments left, and the placenta, which furnished the oxygen and nutritional supply through all the weeks of growth, are discharged and all is ready to return to normal in nature's good time.

Much of the anxiety of childbirth in the past and even today is the lack of any clear picture in the minds of young husbands and wives of just what is taking place when their child is born. The mechanics of childbirth demonstrated in charts, models, moving pictures, now coming into use in schools and colleges, show not only the structure of the reproductive system but its operation during birth. Then, too, graphic pictures lessen the anxiety of young parents, and increase their ability to cooperate as every step of labor proceeds.

HOSPITAL ROUTINE

Often the unexpected routine of the entrance into the hospital and its ritual of preparation for delivery are disconcerting if one has not been oriented beforehand; the undressing and being put into a short, back-closing nightgown, the always humiliating enema and bedpan (unless allowed a trip to the bathroom), the pubic shave for the first time in one's life and the thorough cleansing, as with a baby, of all one's personal "parts," as though one weren't grown up. "This is too much!" but it is only half, for in comes your O.B. himself in pursuit of his own job of examination of heart, lungs, blood pressure, exploration inside and outside of pelvic region to see what the mother is up to, and what the baby is up to, and whether his position is what it should be. It is an inescapable routine, bothersome, but part of the show.

In no time at all, with everything moving along properly, mother is bundled into the delivery room and husband is whisked off to the father's room to join the ranks of expectant fathers. There are two kinds of husbands, and they are both nice! They are just different. There are those who "have their babies" with their wives, as in the ancient folk custom of the cuvada when the fathers went to bed too and received the gifts and tributes of friends. These are the husbands who stand by and lend their good strong arms to every seizure as it comes. "Honey, I wish I could take a few of those for you." And then there are the others whose "business takes them out of town for a day or two." There are not many of these escapers, and they are not so heartless as they seem. The whole business is just too much for them. If they didn't care, they wouldn't need to escape. They are usually good husbands and fathers, but just plain frightened males.

THE CHILDLESS COUPLE

If their physician is the best friend of an expectant young couple, he is also the best friend of other young couples who would like to be expectant, too, but have become discouraged. "What's the matter with us, aren't we human?" they cry out in their hearts, each one loath to blame the other, but more than loath to locate the deficiency within himself.

Traditionally, even today, to some degree, women were asked to accept without question the stigma of "barrenness" placed upon them through the ages, while their husbands were permitted to go free without question. What is more, the man without issue was allowed to "put away" his wife and provide himself with another. Perhaps, for his comfort, he followed vaguely a kind of gardener's reasoning; whereas he had contributed his seed, his wife had, in addition to her own, the great second contribution of the enveloping earth, the environment—hers was the double chance of failure.

Actual knowledge of the sperm and the ovum were delayed until the advent of the microscope, yet even then, when a drop of semen on a slide would throw much light on the fertility or infertility in a given case the husbands were reluctant to submit to the test, partly, no doubt, for fear it might do damage to their long-unchallenged virility. Deficiency in considerable numbers of sperm cells in a given specimen, inferiority in size and form, and failure to attain the normal rate of motility are significant signs indicating infertility. Further investigation might reveal a blocking in the seminal ducts carrying the semen, a condition not too difficult to correct. For the quality and scarcity of sperm cells, hormone treatment has been used, but results have not been too encouraging. Each man should find his own specialist and give him a chance to work on the problem as he sees it.

Because of the many and varying factors bearing on infertility in women, its diagnosis and treatment are much more complicated than in the case of men, but fortunately more effective in results. Their efforts pay off with a much larger percentage of success. Treatment for women involves pelvic exploration of all sorts, including numerous laboratory tests, the taking of temperature records to determine the characteristics of the menstrual cycle, the regularity or vagaries of ovulation, the possible but improbable capture of a live ovum, and fragments of the uterine membrane, and, of course, the condition of the many reproductive passages—tubes, cervix, vagina—with their secretions.

Opening up the Fallopian tubes in case of blockage, supplementing appropriate female sex hormone dosages to meet deficiency secretions when present, together with vigorous amounts of nutritional substances, is the present major course of therapy. Difficult as it is to accept the fact of one's reproductive incapacity after all efforts have failed, it is the only mature, balanced attitude to take. Then, should nature change her ways, give us a surprise, and throw her support in favor of fertility, a relaxed and happy state of mind would help and even promote a surer successful outcome to a belated pregnancy.

Someone tells a story of rare occurrence, where search for causes of their childless state revealed both husband and wife unquestionably infertile. Faced with the double handicap they discontinued treatments, settled down to console each other with their own love and devotion, when, to the surprise of everyone—physicians, friends and themselves most of all—conception took place and carried through to a successful delivery! Why? The answer is one we had better not hazard. Yet, it points up the strength of those mysterious forces, as yet unrevealed or reached by science, that illusive something that evades the mind but obeys the spirit of man.

Similar in its psychic interpretation is the belated pregnancy that often takes place when the infertility of a wife has been long established and the couple has at last adopted a baby. Who is to say what forces awakened to initiate the long-dormant capacity for procreation except that magical spirit of maternity which is the age-old by-product of the care, handling, and cuddling of a child in one's arms.

BABIES FOR ADOPTION

So many are the hospitals, homes, and adoption centers filled with fatherless, motherless babies and young children one can see no justification for a sorrowing, childless home. Yet, even if a young couple is qualified on all points, it is not easy for most men to consent to foster another man's child. Women have a lesser biological ego, they are baby-hungry and another woman's baby has an appeal not lessened, but increased because of its motherlessness.

Resistance to adoption of a child is specially strong (though perhaps unrecognized) in those men who have submitted to tests and found themselves the deficient one of the marriage partnership. Sensitive, they are reluctant to place the seal openly upon their sexual incompetence. As an alternative, infertile husbands are more readily taking advantage of the therapeutic measure of artificial insemination by an unknown donor. With the identity of his wife also unknown to the donor, and knowledge of the whole ceremony deeply buried in the files of the attending physician, the sterile husband has little to fear from public awareness. The child is his legally through his wife and will bear his name without future action. Furthermore, it is carefully linked to both parents through selection of a donor possessing personal traits—hair, eyes, complexion, stature—similar to those of the parents, all carefully noted, typed, matched, much as blood types are matched from blood donors, so that best results may be assured.

For the infertile husband, or for that matter, for the fertile one, who, because of long absences or other reasons has not been able to father a child, therapeutic insemination is a godsend. Objections to it on moral grounds, and the recent legal action of the Supreme Court in ruling against it, seem to me without foundation. Its use is to the progressive and open-minded person entirely comparable to the accepted use of an unknown donor's blood, or segment of skin, or nerve or bone, for relief of human need and welfare. Already storage banks are available to those who in strict secrecy and under medical supervision come to the rescue of the childless. The first institute of research for the perfection of this new contribution to the science of human insemination has been established at the University of Iowa and is making careful progress with anticipated success.

Delayed Parenthood

We cannot leave this subject of parenthood without a word for those young couples who for various reasons—finances, illness, wife employment or the very wise postponement of a pregnancy during the first year of marriage—still need to live close to each other through the sexual bond. Contraception is the prevention of conception by use of a device that blocks the passage of the sperm cells at the entrance into the uterus. It has become not only the resource of the newly married in behalf of a wiser and fuller family planning, but is also the preserver of health and happiness in those marriages in which too-abundant child-bearing could bring damage not only to the mother's health, but to the personal relationship of wife and husband.

The science of contraception still has a few opponents. We cannot answer those who are opposed for religious reasons, but we can answer those who are opposed on moral grounds. They fear that the sanction of contraception will increase promiscuity by removing the danger of illegitimate pregnancy which they consider a common deterrent. Long before the present medically sponsored contraceptive was available many thoroughly unreliable measures had been used. What humanity wants, it wants, and neither laws, nor morals, nor availability stop it. It contrives makeshifts and it uses makeshifts—until it gets something better. The present-day hygienic, carefully designed, contraceptives were welcomed by a waiting and grateful public who needed just such a medically sanctioned instrument to come to the aid of women and children and fathers, too, who were suffering from haphazard, oversized families and all the consequent ills.

For the irresponsible young couple, out for sex experience, the alternative to a reliable contraceptive is the tragic outcome of a possible illegitimate child and/or, frequently, an illegitimate abortion. Physicians who habitually serve in inducing abortions are usually outcasts from the medical profession, if indeed they were ever members of it. Because these men operate hastily, unskillfully, and without regard for the laws of sanitation and hygiene governing surgery, the mortality rate of their patients is extremely high. Eight thousand girls annually pay with their lives. They also pay with their dollars enormous sums of "blood money" which most young boys and girls are driven to extremes to find.

Even in skillful hands whatever is given orally or hypodermically sufficient to interrupt pregnancy is also sufficient to do much physical harm to the patient, who, if she survives, faces the burden of a lifelong sense of guilt with its inevitable degradation and disintegration of character. Physicians in good standing will perform abortions only when the life and serious ill health of the mother is involved. It is in every instance to them a last resort.

The science of gynecology and obstetrics with its conservation of mothers and potential mothers in the conduct of pregnancy, both before and after the hospital experience, is one of the great medical achievements of the day. But the reduction of childbirth mortality is no greater in importance than the far-reaching psychological values which the medical profession is recognizing and fostering. Through education in the first principles of child care and emotional growth, young parents are being prepared to return to their homes equipped to some degree to carry on the hospital's professional standards in both physical and emotional spheres. "I have brought your baby safely into the world," modern doctors are saying, in effect. "You two young parents take him on, from here. The outcome rests with you."

Chapter IX

Education Does It

EDUCATION is a big word. It stands for big things. Even before their children are born fathers and mothers are planning their education. "We want them to have the best there is." You don't question these parents. You know and they know education is preparation for living. It is food, clothing, shelter, and much besides.

What most of us have not realized is that this very education which brings to mind books, teachers, and classrooms, actually begins with mealtime, bedtime, anytime, all times from the very first day when our babies draw their first breath of life and look at us with their funny misty little eyes.

The art of living together in a family, formally "Family Life Education," and the art and science of love and human reproduction, "Sex and Marriage Education," have formed a working partnership in the field of general education and have become modified and changed with new principles and concepts. Remember the spinach-or-nothing era, which now has evolved into "baby knows best"; the corporal-punishment-and-woodshed era which has become a living-room counsel in the best democratic manner, "to talk things "over"; the learning-by-rote era, which has given way to "projects and activities"; the parental-authority era, "because I say so!" now lost in the development of self-direction and self-discipline, to say nothing of the vanishing apology-and-confession which now are considered "futile ends to make amends"?

Can't we all hear daily testimony to the effectiveness of these changes, which have brought home the principle that only change is permanent? What was accepted as right yesterday may be wrong tomorrow. What was wrong yesterday may be right today. Yet, when it comes to family life and sex education we grow resistant and conservative. Here we are touching upon manners and morals, the very fibre of family and personal integrity. Here we change slowly. Yet, observation of the children and young people themselves, and the effect upon those who have experienced the teaching in this new field of education, the over-all benefit in temper and temperament and marriage fitness, have carried it on to a wider and wider acceptance of new ideas and conduct patterns between the sexes.

MARRIAGE EDUCATION

Because this book is dedicated in purpose to the marriage relationship, may we break away from the more comprehensive aspects of family life, and center on education for marriage? Oddly enough, education for marriage, which is an adult affair, begins in early childhood, and falls into four interrelated groupings:

1. The sex education of young children—a factual and "psychic" daily-life foundation;
2. The sex and social development of young teenagers;
3. A deeper understanding of love and marriage requirements;
4. Marriage counseling—an immediate approach for those to be married.

Marriage counseling offers both prenuptial and postnuptial services, which seek to bring about and maintain emotional and physical harmony in the marital relationship.

Through all the four age levels, each with its specific requirements and interests, sex teaching goes forward on two parallel and finally merging themes—the biologic and the psychic—to the end of a matured and balanced libido or sexual self. In an earlier chapter we presented a detailed chart and discussion of the developing stages of the psychic side of the love impulse and its value in an interpretation of the whole marriage relationship. The chapter is offered to young parents in directing the sex guidance and education of their children. Yet the purpose of this chapter is not to rewrite even in outline all that has been recommended as appropriate to a sex education program for young children either at home or at school. It is merely to point the way and indicate a few of the special concerns that frequently get lost in the larger picture. Of hundreds of questions gathered directly from children and their mothers, four have been found to be basic to their own understanding of human reproduction and are most frequently asked. The first concerns maternity:

"Where did I come from?";

the second, birth:

"How did I get out?";

the third, fertilization:

"How did I get started?";

and the fourth, the subject of mating:

"How did the father help start the baby?"

The age that a child approaches this matter depends largely upon circumstance. The questions may come spontaneously or they may come in response to situations at home or in the neighborhood. "Mommie, did Mrs. Gilbert buy her baby at the hospital?" Everything counts as a question and all questions should be answered—not too fully, not too formally, for children like to get things piecemeal and not have them come to the end too fast. They set the pace, we conform.

For detailed discussion of the subject and techniques I should like to refer you to the new editions of my book for parents *New Patterns in Sex Teaching* (1951) and one for children *Being Born* (1954), both published by Appleton-Century-Crofts.

SEX CONDUCT IN PREADOLESCENCE

As for the effect of sex education on children, one can but answer, "Look at the children!"—their expressions, their voices, their attitudes, their manners, when a subject of sex significance occurs spontaneously at home or at school. It affects them as any interesting legitimate subject would affect them. The restless shuffling, the covert glances, the giggling that used to betray their inner feelings are all but gone. Outside, among themselves, for fun, there are the usual jokes and stories but these among children are something else, with an interpretation all their own. Real conduct and play conduct, real motives and make-believe motives are easily confused. Yet parents are logical when they are concerned about "experimenting" as the follow-up of sex teaching. All other subjects, they know, are rounded out and made to live in a child's mind through projects and experiences. The same is true of the teaching of reproduction, human and subhuman. He wants to see! He wants to watch when the puppies are born or when Mommie feeds the new baby. Why not? The world is full of life in the making at every turn.

How about the nearest farm where the children can see, at the proper season, whole pastures of young calves, lambs, colts with their mothers? Or there are sure to be somewhere in the neighborhood mother cats hiding their kittens or carrying them about in their mouths to a new retreat, or a "lady dog" who is being taken to the "vet" so that she won't have puppies. As for fertilization, it also can best be illustrated on the farm by opening a fertile egg. The drama of life's beginnings is almost impossible to escape in the appearance of the fuzzy little chick embryo. The story of birth even comes to the screen these days with Walt Disney's pictures of stream, desert, and forest—an enriching and developing experience. Linked together in the active minds of children, the scheme of the universe and life itself cannot help taking on form and meaning. Inwardly, the children accept the whole, not because they understand it all—who does?—but because it answers something within them which they instinctively feel is great, thrilling, and real.

This lifting of the curtain, this giving meaning to the world of living things about them, has done something else for children. It has changed over from the debit to the credit side of conduct a whole category of play and make-believe among boys and girls which once were considered wrong, including make-believe keeping house, having babies, nursing babies, undressing each other, going swimming. There was a time when all spontaneous activities of the remotest sex import were taboo for children, not only taboo, but considered precocious, abnormal, "oversexed," perverse —no words were too condemnatory, no punishment too drastic. Modesty began in the cradle, and sex segregation in bathroom soon after. Today, nursery school etiquette allows little boys to escort little girls to the toilet and permits them to help each other in the casual manner of little sisters and big brothers at home.

This gradual introduction to the differences in body build in the sexes, and its later interpretation in functioning as father and mother, serves its good purpose not only in the days of childhood but in the marriage situation ahead. "Why are little boys and girls different from each other?" "Little boys are growing up to be fathers; little girls are growing up to be mothers. Each has a different part to play." Such answers do not promote misconduct; lack of straightforward answers often do. Children are willing to wait to grow up. "Can I be a father someday? Can I be a mother when I'm a big girl?" Sex education gives fair assurance of good conduct. It is the promise of things to come, things close to the heart of every child no matter how young. After sex teaching none of the tragic fears of old need come to wreck a happy honeymoon and marriage.

On the emotional and affectionate side, the public is still wary and largely uninformed, still inclined to interpret in harsh terms the tender developing love interests of their children. Yet accepted guidance principles recognize that changing love attractions are part of the whole developing pattern of the sex impulse, which for honest growth must be permitted normal legitimate expression at each stage. Fear, prohibitions, jealousies, overprotection, suspicions tend to block the outward moving stream of the impulse and leave it crippled and retarded. Sex education fosters mutual attraction between boys and girls, early dating in suitable surroundings, and first expressions of a love interest. Thanks to these teachings, fewer blockages are occurring along the pathway to mature sex development today, fewer men and women are remaining unwed. For more detail in this field I should like to make mention of my book, *The Normal Sex Interests of Children,* Appleton-Century-Crofts, N. Y., 1948.

Adolescent Preparation

If preparation for marriage in childhood seems a bit forehanded, in adolescence, with its new sex functioning and awakened libido, it becomes more appropriate and timely. In adolescence the interest focuses largely on the dramatic changes themselves, which create

Alice-in-Wonderland surprises in bodily fullness and broadness and in personality as well. Closer even to their hearts lies the interest in sex maturing. Teenagers may yield to fate or inheritance, an inch or two in height or a pound or two in weight, but when it comes to sex development, they demand 100% delivery with no margin of loss. Yet it is difficult to set standards. No area of bodily mechanism, the gynecologist tells us, shows greater variation than the sexual in both boys and girls even within normal functioning limits.

Certainly any significant variation in size or forms of genitalia, or absence (as in the case of undescended testicles), should be brought to a specialist's attention as soon as observed, as well as any marked pubertal delay. Children are sensitive, self-conscious, and worrisome about these things. Quite as important as the actual correction of any difficulty is the sense of relief experienced and the prevention of the personality changes that so frequently accompany sexual variations. For years a young girl would not room with another girl or stay overnight with her friends, not because she was modest but because her breasts were too small. The idea of smallness had been given to her by her mother who began to pad her dresses when she was twelve.

Few are the girls today who are not prepared for the advent of menstruation either by their mothers or by the nurses at school, though perhaps more boys would be left to find their way alone if it were not for the physical education director. Best of all is the understanding this mutual knowledge of each other affords the young husband and wife when they enter upon their close association in marriage.

SEX ATTRACTION

The young adolescent must learn to woo, but he must not be a wooer; he must learn to sue, but he must not be a suitor; he must learn to be a husband, but have no wife. He reminds us of the old nursery rhyme, "How can he eat without any knife? How can he marry without a wife?"

The safety of the young adolescent lies in numbers, because the safety of his marriage choice lies in numbers. Shopping around is not promiscuity at fourteen, fifteen, sixteen. Shopping around is good business. Boys must meet and date many girls; girls meet and date many men not to "brush the down from the peach," as our parents used to say, but to learn to know each other. Those who do marriage counseling find that permanence in marriage is strengthened by these early excursions, this broad dating in the teens; lack of it brings trouble.

Much of the resistance parents feel toward broad early dating is found in their concern over the ever-

present custom of petting and its more serious counterpart in the background, the premarital relationship.
Yet, touch activities are as much preparation for marriage as the dating that brings them about, and the
young teen-ager is as impelled to touch, stroke, and
caress as the little three-year-old he was ten or more
years before. In both cases the impulse is instinctive,
involuntary at first, but purposeful on nature's part,
who is getting her children ready to be mating men
and women.

Yet, here nature's laws and man's laws come violently
into conflict and the familiar "don't touch!", "don't
pet" training begins. Society must have known that
it was opposing nature's own plans, else it would not
have enforced its own so violently. No other childish
misconduct has been more severely punished than
sex misconduct. What society did not know was that in-
stinct "nipped in the bud" fails to come to full flower
when society decides that it may. Lack of response
in love and marriage, the touch-me-not frigid wife,
the impotent man, and, more frequently in the past
than now, the celibate—the unmarried in large numbers, these were the results of the "don't touch" training. And now?

Now it is that parents may lose their fears in the assurance that nature herself has provided her young immature adult with her own safeguards. The young teen-
ager is neither full-blown in his sexual capacity, nor

full-blown in his lovemaking. He is tentative, shy, exploring. He runs away from his interest, comes back again. Not until the middle or late teens does he come to full flower biologically and then, modified by circumstance and reason, he begins on his own to temper the stronger drive. Greatest and most reliable of all guides is education, which in its own unique, penetrating fashion develops within each person his own code of ethics. This is no psychological theory. It is the findings of those who have made the most reliable study of sex morals. To foster sex education is to foster sex morality.

PIN-UP GIRLS AND NUDES

Another one of the marriage preparatory activities of the young adolescent, in this instance the male, is his interest in pin-up girls, both nude and partly nude. Yet the pursuit of the beautiful "Pin-Up," we must admit, is vastly different from, shall we say, that of the old gentleman at the Follies? The old gentleman is seeking what he has lost, the young adolescent what he hopes to gain. His interest is a mixture of learning to know and of anticipation of experience, once removed. To a young developing male, a female is to be seen, to be brought into one's horizon, later to be married, loved, and possessed. All of this, is seems to me, must be borne in mind when one appraises the universal attraction of men for the pin-up girl. If they wanted the real thing they could find her. The pin-up is their substitute.

MARRIAGE EDUCATION

Although sex education in the long-range sense is preparation for marriage, it is not marriage education in the technical sense, nor is it marriage counseling. Sex education (lest any casual reader has become bewildered) is addressed to those below marriage age. Marriage education is for everyone who is looking toward married life, and counseling for those who, having made their choice, are ready for immediate pre-nuptial preparation. The whole structure of education for marriage and family life is like a four-tiered wedding cake which begins with a broad substantial base, narrows in as it grows taller and tops off at the peak with a sugary little bride and groom on a platform made for two.

The strongest advocates of marriage education are those who have tried it. It is a favorite course in senior high schools and colleges where young engaged couples like to attend together, sitting side by side, hands locked, as they did by the hundreds in Dr. Noel Keys' classes at the University of California in Berkeley for many years. "We are keeping our lecture notes," one of these senior girls said. "We don't ever expect to need a lawyer."

Premarital Counseling

The modern bride and groom, especially those who have had marriage education and know its value, are increasingly adding counseling to their prenuptial preparations. Because there is a medical checkup required by law before the issue of a marriage license (chiefly as a prevention against the spread of venereal disease), many doctors have come to double as examining physician and counselor. It is a natural union of services and saves the second contact with another person. It is also a step toward the requirement of a more detailed pelvic examination for brides and grooms in the interest of fertility, with an added mental health examination to determine the emotional fitness of a marrying couple. Lest this be not enough, follow-up free pamphlets are offered on every hand—at the City Hall where young couples go to get their licenses, at the doctor's office where a notice says, "Take One," and at the minister's study where they lie at hand in an inviting little pile. As one young fellow said, showing his collection to a buddy, "They sure are not taking a chance on our going A. W. O. L."

Of the premarriage trilogy which unites law, medicine, and the clergy, the doctor's role is the most significant, when it combines, as it should, the services of both physician and counselor. Rarely is there a man or woman of any age who is able to approach marriage without feelings of uncertainty and fearsome-

ness, and in many instances with lingering traces of
hidden guilt for lapses in chastity or doubts of sexual
fitness. These tangible and intangible records do not,
everyone knows, escape the searching eye of the physician. He goes where neither law nor clergy can go. He
helps where neither can help.

The question is bound to arise, shall the prospective
husband and wife consult the same physician or shall
each consult separately? If the physician chosen is
trustworthy and professionally equipped, I see every
reason for keeping together and sharing his skill. But
this physician should be a specialist in his field, a
gynecologist with psychiatric training as it applies to
the marriage situation. For he (or she) is not only the
agent of the state in fulfillment of requirements for a
license to marry, but he is ethically the custodian of
this marriage, as he passes on the total fitness of the
young partners.

The law requires three days to give formal sanction
to a marriage in the issuance of a license. Three weeks
or more would be better for many reasons. Medically,
aside from the venereal tests, there can be pelvic situations that need correction, a tough hymen, a hooded
clitoris, some adverse condition of vagina or cervix or
whatnot—minor difficulties which need more than
three days to correct. Emotionally (and when isn't it
"emotionally"?), three days is as nothing, and the
shortness of the interval is likely to produce panic, if
there are inner conflicts and tensions. These, your good

physician-counselor will reassuringly resolve, but not in three days. Yet, miraculously, even on the first day anxieties begin to lessen.

For the young bride they begin to lessen when, like a child, she begins to speak of, to touch, to explore her known but unfamiliar self. She learns the long-unspoken names and the location of the parts of her own reproductive mechanism and their functions—vulva, vagina, cervix, uterus, Fallopian tubes, ovaries—that invisible and miraculous labyrinth of nature's workshop for the production of human beings. The accent, the meaning of it all changes. This is not "sex," the old forbidden, this is marriage, husband, home, babies, the longed-for, the revered. And, as the learning goes on, through the talk and the handling of the plastic models so exactly a replica of her own reproductive self, other barriers are lowered and personal anxieties and uncertainties come to the fore. "What about a broken membrane? Is it a sign of loss of virginity? How can there be such a thing as circumcision for girls? What would make a girl frigid? Would it be giving yourself away to respond to your husband?"

Girls who have attended marriage classes know the answers to these "hearsay" fragments of old wives' tales, and are long-since familiar with both male and female reproductive systems, through charts, films, and other audio-visual aids. They have learned that the membrane, or hymen as it is called, which stretches across the opening to the vagina is never entirely intact, but must have openings to permit the menstrual discharge. Today, the vigorous, athletic activities of girls often destroy the whole thing. Only vestiges are left. Think, how could the popular tampon be inserted without perforations? So the state of the hymen has no value at all as a sign of virginity. Circumcision for girls? There are analogous parts in the basic sex structure of males and female. The male penis has its counterpart in girls in a tiny organ called the clitoris. Both are organs of great sensitiveness with many nerve endings. They are the source of the peculiar sensation in intercourse which is called climax or orgasm. In both men and women, a little hood of skin normally covers the organ. The cutting away of this cup of skin in both boys and girls is called circumcision, though commonly only boys are circumcised and for different reasons: religious, hygienic, and sexual. As to what would make a girl frigid, or a boy for that matter, we must refer you back to Chapter II. Frigidity has many causes: sex antagonism—"My father was so mean to my mother"; sex revulsion—"I can't bear to be touched"; fear of pregnancy—"We can't afford any more children"; emotional states of all sorts, anger, resentment, suspicion—"There's somebody else"; all of these and many more are found to bring about frigidity, which is practically always of psychic origin. Often it is traceable to childhood conditioning—a consistent teaching or atmosphere of sex rejection—sometimes to later periods of tension between husband

and wife. Men as well as women are subject to "sex conditioning"—all are extremely sensitive to rejection or to the opposite, to aggressiveness, which may throw them completely off balance—"Look—whose party is this?" Because men are dependent upon their own powers of erection for the achievement of coitus, they must be left to their own rhythmic set for the united experience, which, however is not inflexible and unadaptable.

The correction of frigidity is not a matter of force, not a matter of will power, it is a matter of the removal of the cause that has brought about the emotional blocking. Taking sedatives or other drugs to help is not only artificial but false to the whole situation. One cannot counterfeit love, and love, together with a relieved mind, will bring the desired response. It is during this emotional re-education in which confidence and knowledge have been increasing that all kinds of hidden secrets come to confession in further questions.

"Should all sex experiences be confessed, even those in childhood?"

"Should one or two affairs in high school be confessed?"

"Would a doctor know whether a girl had had a baby?"

"Would he let her know he knew?"

It is not easy to be someone else's conscience but any good counseling physician will tell his patient what has seemed to work out best in most cases. No one needs to confess a childhood experience, or even a later one if it has not built up an obsessive sense of guilt or a frigidity that must be relieved in order to share his life happily. Few husbands and wives enter marriage without some sex experience, and if asked would probably confess they would rather not have renewed the matter. There are one or two situations, however, that require a complete and entire frankness; that is a previous marriage, with or without a child, or an illegitimate pregnancy. Those are two experiences which have a damaging effect upon a relationship if they are not previously known and accepted.

As to the knowledge of the examining physician, he would undoubtedly know whether a uterus had ever been pregnant. Whether he mentioned it or not would depend very much upon his interpretation of the effect that his knowledge might have upon the girl. He would be influenced by her tenseness, the moisture of her skin, and other physical symptoms of distress. If discussing the matter would not help the present situation, he probably would remain silent. However, if he felt that her silence would interfere with any adjustment within the marriage she was entering upon, he might gradually make tentative approaches toward opening up the subject of her girlhood pregnancy in order to forestall a real unhappiness should her secret be revealed. Whether a physician would let the patient know or not concerning detected former pregnancy, the obligation is upon her to make confession of it to the man she marries, whether it came to a successful or abortive close.

Sex education, marriage education, marriage counseling are a progressive series of study, of living, and of learning ranging over usually a whole twenty-year span—longer than a medical course, longer than an engineering course, longer than training for any other profession—yet the rewards in each case and the total number of cases which would follow through this education could not but make for us a new world of marriage permanence, a new world of married happiness.

Chapter X

Time of Crisis

SITTING near a group of young people one day, I caught a protesting voice. "Why are they always telling us what is wrong with marriage? Why doesn't someone tell us what is right? Or isn't there any right?"

It was hard not to break in and answer this protest. Of course there is right in marriage and there will be more that is right the longer we work at it. Marriage today is like the bridge out there on the edge of my town. It has served many generations but it is giving way and is being replaced by a new one. Meanwhile, the sign "Caution, bridge under construction," destroys confidence in both the old and the new. It is the same with marriage. The old is wavering. The new is not yet tested and assured.

Yet, marriage as it is taking form today has real potentials. It has possibilities lying within it as never before. Husbands and wives are meeting on all levels —economic, domestic, sexual, educational. His work, his gains and losses, his successes and defeats are hers. Her gains and losses are also his, granting that she has (as more and more she does have) a business apart from his. The home, the children—their rearing, their education, their recreation—are a father's new avocation. He is becoming more maternal and domestic, gathers his brood more closely under his wings, pets and punishes while he is becoming definitely father in act as well as fact.

The marital relationship outstrips them all in the unexpectedness and swiftness of its progress toward a long-cherished ideal of oneness in heart, mind, and body, achieved, one is forced to admit, not by way of the old, but by the new bridge with its new kind of love supports and its mutual contributions.

But all of this requires the seasoning of time and the skill of experience before it will carry us along as contented and confident travelers. A little lady of the past generation who said, "The women will go along with you but the men won't," is speaking out of her own era. Men of today are not attempting to take away from women their new recognition and freedom. They know their value, but everyone, men included, wants to make sure that homes and households do not suffer, neither mother herself, father himself, nor the children.

Everyone, those who are marrying and those who are not, needs orientation and education in marriage's structure and operation. Marriage is a new technology with many details to be worked out and foreseen both by the onlookers—the public, the parents—and by those most intimately concerned, the participants. There is no precedent for the type of marriage evolving today. That is why so much has been written about the mistakes, about "what is wrong" rather than "what is right"—why, that is, it has been carrying a sign, "Go slow . . . bridge under construction."

The New Alliance

The changes that are transforming marriage from a hall-marked institution with established rites and ceremonies into an individual, self-starting, self-regulating affair are here and neither ask nor accept quarter from anyone. "We are marrying each other," today's bride and groom say, "not each other's families." It all sounds like a sudden transition, but it has been building up a long time. Marriage is also more personal today so far as individual demands are concerned. The choose-your-own pattern makes it so, when the older standards of suitability in age, social and financial standing, and so on have been discarded. The husband may be the good provider, the good caretaker always required; the wife may be the good mother and homemaker. But if either fails to square with the other's personal requirements, disappointments, frictions, hurts arise. The demand is for a you-and-me relationship, no matter how many "of us" there come to be, counting the children—three, four, five. "Forsaking all others," the marriage ritual says, and they agree with the ritual.

But there is a generally unknown, unrecognized factor that influences the carrying out of this you-and-me relationship. A couple may be entirely to each other's liking—personal qualities, tastes, interests, congeniality of temperament, age, religion, race, and all the rest made to order, with, of course, a strong underlying pervasive and persuasive love. You think it can't go wrong. But the ceremony at the altar which makes two persons legally, socially, and publicly man and wife sets them into a totally new relationship involving the opening up of unforeseen personality traits. More than outer circumstances, more than personal factors, there are unexpected motivating forces which the new circumstances of marriage call forth and which must be acknowledged, understood, and intelligently met if the marriage is to succeed.

With marriage counseling, marriage classes and studies increasing in the colleges, the present generation of men and women will create a new type of marriage suited to a new type of world, economically, socially, sexually speaking. They are not only making a study of the arts and sciences involved in marriage itself, but each is studying it in terms of the individual's and his partner's psychological requirements. Love, they are determined, shall no longer be blind or subservient, and need not be, still to be love.

Love's Identity

"How do you know it's love?" The initial question of all young people comes spontaneously, searchingly, in perpetual repetition. No matter what the answer gathered from instructor's notebook or poet's verse or author's lines, they still pursue some nebulous but fixed ideal. *This* is love . . . but how does one know?

Yet, each person's "this"—his concept—is his alone. For love is not the same for all persons, and is not static. Just as right is not always right, nor wrong always wrong, so love is not always love. It changes. Within marriage, after the public ritual and actual possession—"I, John, take thee, Mary . . . "—love is different, deeper, closer than even that of the engagement period, still different from that of the courtship days. The changing aspects of love in these deepening relationships are the joy, the excitement, the adventure of love. Love is the handmaiden of the procreative or reproductive self. It is the psychic accompaniment, the blending of minds and hearts, which draws a man and a woman together in a feeling of inner oneness and completion. Love is the ornamental, esthetic side of marriage which so strengthens and deepens the union that it survives after the reproductive years are passed, yes, even when they have been fruitless. When a marriage has not been productive—not in children, or economic or domestic competence, or health—when all of the essential requirements have been lacking, and love still holds, one knows it to be true. Did anyone think those four words "for richer for poorer" applied only to dollars? Every day we see them applied to love. No, love is not static. It changes, it becomes richer and poorer, strengthens or declines, lives or dies during the years of its keeping in our hands.

Because of the various aspects of love's expression, the identification of it is difficult. An assertive, volatile person readily wins his girl over the unassertive, inarticulate one whose capacity for satisfying the requirements of marriage are many times greater. Recalling the inhibiting effects of certain drastic childhood teaching concerning petting and lovemaking, we can readily understand the handicap of some young people when in rivalry with those less restrained. Another, even more frequent injustice is suffered when, in pursuit of the lost satisfactions of childhood or adolescence, one's motives and even one's loyalty are challenged.

A young woman who after marriage blossomed into a veritable American beauty found herself the object of a masculine admiration never matched in her somewhat drab girlhood. As the glances and wolf-calls followed her, she began overaccenting both the style and color of her dress, visited public places with and without her husband, who had little effect upon the succession of whistles and calls.

Affronted, resentful at the perpetual disregard for his rights, husbandly protests and accusations became perpetual. "Tone down your looks or go by yourself, like a common—"

"Don't say it! You have no right to say it!"

"You have no right to act it."

"But it doesn't mean anything. It's just my fun, my vanity. It does something for me. Don't make it what it is not! Please, Rudy!"

But Rudy could not 'please.' She didn't care, he maintained. How could she care and sacrifice his feelings? What must those fellows think of him? He knew what they thought, and they were right, so far as she was concerned.

In the end, the wife yielded. The game wasn't worth the candle. She loved her husband. Psychologically, hers was a choice, not between husband and other men, but between husband and self. This girl was filling in the long overdue teen-age popularity with boys. But when her husband reacted so strongly that she was in danger of losing him, the old craving was sacrificed to the great present issue, and girl became wife once more.

More frequent but less spectacular are the little day-by-day episodes which put love to the test. Women resent casualness or any apparent or genuine neglect more readily than men. Their sense of values is different. The immediate specific act often serves as a gauge or indicator of masculine devotion. "I couldn't do a thing like that to anyone I love," a girl exclaimed, after some characteristic bit of husbandly absent-mindedness. No, perhaps she couldn't, but he could, and not from lack of love.

A very young husband who knew little about wives and less about pregnancy had arranged to meet his wife at his office, one noon, to sign some important papers. By noon, the street had become a glare of ice.

"Darling, I don't believe I'd better come down this noon," she telephoned.

"Why not?"

"It's so slippery." (Surely he hadn't forgotten!)

"Slippery! Don't be a softie. Put on some rubbers and get going. It's important."

Indignant, resentful, hurt, the young wife slipped and slid the few blocks to her husband's office. How could he forget? He didn't care.

But of course, he did care very much, as their long, happy life together proved over and over again. What this young wife did not know was that, for the moment, her pregnancy had indeed been crowded out of his mind by the business of the hour. Such are the constantly recurring trifles which in the early married years bring about hurt feelings and doubts of love's full measure. To meet them, they must be appraised, not as one incident or even as several incidents, certainly not according to one's own code, but in light of the specific person concerned. A chivalrous husband is not more devoted than one who lets his wife carry in the laundry. He is just better trained. The wife who bakes her husband's favorite dish once a week loves him no more than one who doesn't.

So we return to the perennial question: What is love? We have tossed the ball around, but we have not made a basket. Biologically, psychologically, love between men and women is a compound of sex and psychic attraction with varying degrees of each as a contributing source. It has been said by some that the sex drive is stronger in men; the psychic stronger in women. That depends upon the individual person, his natural endowments and his cultural delevopment. Those in a position to know claim no sex advantage. The capacity to love is about equal in any case with individual variations.

THE SEX SIDE

In discussing the sex life of primitive peoples, anthropologists tell us that some of them have no word for love. We wonder. Does this mean there's no word because there's no counterpart in their experience? And what, we wonder, does lack of love do to the marital relationship? Leaves it where it always has been, no doubt—a routine, domestic association.

Civilization has brought us a long way. The sex side of marriage for most of us is far from being a routine incident, however much the marriage fluctuates between domesticity and romance. Sex in marriage is a significant part of it, above and beyond its original purpose of procreation. But, because of the dual quality of the sexual impulse, the growth and significance of the psychic elements surrounding and enriching the native reproductive drives, the two have come into balance, the reproductive side being the inner mechanism, the heart; the psychic being the life blood which bring vitality to the whole. The psychic forces give marriage depth and radiance. When the sex factor is withdrawn for reasons of illness, absence, mental and emotional stress, but love remains intact, the marriage holds. As one young husband said, faced with a virgin existence, "It does not matter that much. What matters is Mary." But let love be withdrawn, the sexual relationship follows and the marriage perishes.

The fundamentals in acquiring technique and harmony in the attainment of a balanced marital relationship have been the subject of so many studies and writings on marriage that there need to be no repetition here. Dr. Abraham Stone's revised manual, Dr. Ernest Burgess and Dr. Wallin's *New Engagement and Marriage*, and many other books mentioned in the reading list supply rich and reliable suggestions. I leave you to them, and them to you.

NEED FOR SCRUTINY

With the increase in sex education and tolerance, and the "choose-your-own" wife or husband custom, why do so many find themselves in a sea of marital discontent, their marriages struggling for survival? Remember the bridge of transition and the sign, "Go slow"? Let a young married speak. "We thought we were in love. We went steady all through high school. We enjoyed each other. We hadn't thought much about marriage, but one day we decided to go along with another couple, friends of ours. Now we doubt that we ever were really in love. We get on each other's nerves. There doesn't seem to be anything left. Nobody cares."

This young couple represent hundreds, yes, if the truth were told, thousands of young people. Their marriage has counterparts all over the country. School days were over. The boy had a job, earned a good wage. He was ready to "take a wife" and start a family. His high school steady was the logical choice. He knew no other girl so well. Besides, a certain intimacy and getting used to each other were already accomplished.

Yet the marriage came to grief. It came to grief because of the factors it did *not* have to hold it together. It was too routine; it needed the spark of romance. It was too solid, too uninspired. Knowing one's steady through four susceptible high-school years, no matter how intimately, is not preparation for the choice of a lifetime partner. It is restrictive, develops little basic judgment or knowledge of human conduct. Man-nature, woman-nature are unexplored entities. If married years are to be full and happy, the young teenager should be permitted to experience the searching, expanding, developing associations that will lead to capacity for mature choice and adjustments when de-

cisions are required. Marriage failures give evidence
of the hazards of propinquity, acceptance of the person
at hand, because he is at hand.

There is another frequently disruptive factor in contemporary marriage. Not bird-in-hand availability, it
is almost the opposite in a sense—namely popularity.
Many a young man marries the town belle ("doll"
today) as he is about to leave home after school days
are over, just to keep her for himself, a precaution
against the inroads of rivals. College or business training over, he returns to his love gradually to realize
that their ways have parted, there is no common
ground of interest, no spark of the old attachment. The
dreariness of it all is, nobody is to blame. The estrangement is not for lack of loyalty, but for lack of maturity,
mutual growth toward mutual ends. Sometimes the
dreariness of the change is followed by the unnecessary tragedy of acquiescence, the two remaining
together in spite of their knowledge of incompleteness
and inner withdrawal. Spiritless acquiescence is rarely
justified, it is sometimes even cowardly. Every effort
must be exerted to rekindle even a dead-as-ashes partnership, but when there is nothing left to kindle, acceptance of failure is better than futile struggle or
apathy, for it holds out promise of a new beginning.

Immaturity, youth, idealism, pay heavy tolls at other
points. The inexperienced man, young or not so young,
in the hands of an older woman, working in behalf of
herself or her daughter, is caught in a bewilderment of

confusions. Sometimes inducements are held out quite frankly in terms of financial gain or property settlement. Other women more subtle and not quite honest with themselves foster romance successfully with considerable benefit. The experienced man detects and escapes these available alliances, fearful of their outcome. The inexperienced are captured to their future disillusionment and undoing. A similar but more tragic *mésalliance* is one in which the knowledge of an unexpected handicap of alcoholism, existing marriage, multiple divorce, mental or physical disability has been withheld. A hasty marriage takes place and gradually or suddenly the reality of the situation is revealed.

These are a few of the marriage casualties brought about chiefly by immaturity and lack of firsthand experience which comes from years of interplay between the sexes during the growing-up period. Acquaintance with sex-inspired behavior in the broad educational meaning of the word is sex and marriage preservation.

Now we are wondering what is the forward look in these several situations? Can these marriages be repaired? Do they hold promise of restoration, or shall they be dissolved, or left to drift their dreary way? No one has ready-made answers, but there are too many hundreds and thousands of men and women, living out their negative, passive existences, to leave them without at least some thought for the future.

Of the four marriages of immaturity mentioned, the first two hold greater promise than the second two. The first two possess in common, shall we say, a congenial and spontaneous background of young, but untried, love. This has possibilities of revival. The lagging partner can catch up, study his (or her) deficiencies or excesses and work at their extinction.

The second two were based, in each case, on a cultivated attachment, with underlying motives withheld on the part of the aggressor. A certain sense of guilt on the one hand, and of being taken in, on the other, lessened the chances of a genuine return to any earlier, happier relationship. Take, for example, the women who marry just to have babies and practically ignore their husbands. As many a little five-year-old has asked (or implied), "Mommie, what does that man stay here for?"

A couple who have once loved each other and then have grown apart without special reason tend to stay together until some precipitating cause brings each one face to face with the situation and his part in it. Sometimes it is the marriage of one's children and the greater need for companionship after they have left, or the loss of a parent, the making of a will, the transfer to another city, or the forming of a new partnership. Any one of these new milestones tends to sharpen one's perception and open up closed doors of thought and feeling followed by new evaluations and decisions.

What one finds, what one is willing to look at and act upon will influence or determine the outcome.

A second kind of marriage bankruptcy, the kind in which a man finds himself at the altar without quite knowing why, is a hazardous marriage, one with a doubtful outlook for the future. It has a doubtful outlook because it is a woman-made marriage at a time when women do not yet have the right to make marriage on an equal basis with men. They lack social sanction, which in effect is stronger than legal sanction. Most of all they lack the sanction of men, with whom they are seeking to share an age-old masculine prerogative, the freedom of choice in marriage.

In short, there is a resentment in many a husband's mind against his wife-made marriage which is not felt in the outgrown marriage. But the resentment is lessening as women are demonstrating their right to be more than passive participants in a cooperative partnership.

Marriages of convenience or availability are usually barren of romance. When they fail, the same inexperience that brought them about prevents or hinders a wise and just solution. Girls, more than men, are adept at ending an unhappy alliance, unless they are afraid of not making another. They are less tolerant, less patient, more impulsive. Men are more long-suffering, more chivalrous, more sensitive to public opinion. Even men who have earned their freedom many times over still wait for their erring wives to take the initiative in procuring legal release for them both.

Divorce?

A marriage that had little or nothing to start on in the past and holds little or nothing in the present gives little or no promise for the future. The principals of such a marriage owe it to themselves, their friends, and their family, to bring it to a close. Human life is too short, happiness too rare, unhappiness too destructive in this troubled world, to ask any man or woman to live out together an empty and unproductive existence.

Young children and elderly parents may hold an estranged husband and wife together temporarily under a kind of armed truce, but even such a makeshift must be periodically examined to make sure that those for whom the truce has been made are really being benefited and not, instead, being injured. Whether a couple remains together for the children's sake depends upon their response to the family situation. If the children are greatly attached to both parents, who are able to live amicably without overt accusations and bickerings, holding the family together may be the answer while the children are at home. But if violent scenes are the order of the day, with threats of leaving on the one hand and open recrimination on the other, the effects upon the children may be worse than a clean-cut separation. Children cannot live contentedly nor happily under the constant threat of a disrupting home. The harmful effects are apparent in their instability

and evidences of tension in various disturbing auto-
matisms: nail-biting, stammering, night terrors and
dreams, frequent fears, irritability, and sickness.

Children in the Home

As every married couple knows, children themselves,
one's own or adopted, are frequently the focal point
of differences between parents. Sometimes they are the
original and inciting cause which threatens the whole
family structure; lack of child interest on the part of a
husband—"I'm not a family man"; the matter of adoption—"I don't care for other people's children"; diver-
gences in method of rearing—"She's too soft with the
boy," or, "He's too harsh"; or the all too-familiar over-
attachment of one parent for a child which crowds out
the other—"I don't count any more."

Let's take a look at each of these four psychological
sinners. With all the increased awareness on the part of
the public of the tragic results of being an unwelcome
child, creating one if he is to suffer a lifelong feeling
of rejection, is little short of criminal. Let only those
husbands and wives have babies who wholeheartedly
want them. Were not unwelcome babies lessening in
number, I would, no doubt, be advocating a fantastic
plan of licensing young couples for parenthood, as we
now license them for marriage in the interest of human
welfare. But there is a less drastic measure in the principle of the Planned Parenthood movement with its

teaching that voluntary parenthood is right and involuntary is wrong if a child is to suffer rejection, and they show you what to do about it.

Even greater hazards lie in wait for an adopted child than for one of the parents' own. It is difficult enough to be a stranger without discovering that the new home has but half a welcome. Adopted children require a double amount of assurance in their entrance into a new home. Sensitive to their situation even when they are mere toddlers, they are weather vanes of fluctuating response to their environment. The longer the full acceptance of both parents is delayed, the more trying the situation for everyone.

A father gives a picture of his retreat after years of lost battles. His young son, adopted, not quite assured of his welcome would wait eagerly for his father's return each evening, craving, no doubt, some positive evidence of his acceptance. Father, weary from office work, needing rest and peace after battling traffic would sink into his lounge chair. Then the skirmish would begin: "Dad, help me fix this—Dad, how do you multiply—?Dad, will you take me to a basketball game tonight? Dad, can I have—?" all the time cavorting around the room, acting silly, and making himself a protracted nuisance. That failing, he would shift into high gear, fall over his father's feet, hang over the back of his chair, breathe down his neck, ask for the sports page, until an exasperated father, failing to get any support from the mother, would flee the place and take himself off to sit in the car, with the door locked.

Leaving—parent's leaving or child's leaving—does not take care of the situation for anyone. All children must be accepted and given their rightful place in the family where they find themselves. This requires a definite state of heart and mind translated into the intangible essentials of companionship, interest in their schools, their homes, their friends, their social outlets, all the psychic side of their natures. The time and discipline that it takes to be a good parent, when one didn't want to be a parent at all, is considerable, but it pays off in the end. A man can find real people in his children who, once they feel assured of their rightful place in his home and his affection, will be content, take themselves off and ask only for their share.

There is much anxiety today over young delinquents and the origin of their delinquency. The origin, as Dr. Sheldon Gluck and others have found in their studies, is the indifferent, disunited, shrugging-of-the-shoulders sort of home, the one which sends children forth to take out their resentment with defiance upon a police-ridden world. These young modern marauders will not roll up their sleeves and "take on" their parents within the confines of four walls—we will not call it a home—but they will make for the open and take on a whole community, having cast their fate with other neglected boys.

CHILD MANAGEMENT

A local judge recently shocked, or only surprised, some of his hearers, by passing sentence upon a young culprit of a goodly number of paddle strokes to be administered by his father. "What," an ordinary layman would want to know, "was a child doing in a court of law who could be turned from his misbehavior by a ping-pong paddle? How old was he? Was this just a frightening game for a nursery child?" It reminded me of a four-year-old whose parents some years ago had taken him to court for teasing little girls.

If the present boy were old enough for a court appearance, what sort of judge was this who had so little knowledge of recognized interpretations of delinquency that he would resort to so futile a measure as corporal punishment in any form? Another judge, one from the Family Court Center of Toledo, would have directed this child and his father to its own Child Study Institute in which both of them would have been given equal personal consideration. Woodshed tactics are neither employed nor advocated. Children are neither considered nor called delinquents. Both children and their parents have the right to bring their troubles to the court and to be given impartial, available assistance in time of need.

Hosts of young husbands and wives bring to the rearing and management of their children—especially their first children—the immeasurable distance existing between these two court judges and their methods of child correction. Corporal punishment is a confession of a lack of intelligence in someone; in the child if his parents must resort to measures rarely employed by even animal trainers, in the parent if he has not learned the fundamental rules of child management and must resort to force. More than that, children learn by imitation. The parent who reaches for a weapon—paddle or switch or whatever—to carry out punishment, must be prepared to find his child also reaching for one to supplement his own inadequate strength in times of self-defense.

As a matter of fact, punishment of any sort is a last resort and rarely required if the day-by-day situations have been adequately met. They can be met by those who have not neglected to prepare for the very interesting and specialized profession of becoming a successful parent. The reward comes not only in the greater ease and enjoyment in each other through the growing-up years, but later when the children, grown to mature, balanced adulthood, bear evidence to the wise, intelligent home and parental guidance they have received.

Differences in child management are closely linked to lapses in the personal relationship of husbands and wives. They arise with the children themselves, usually the first baby, as the focal point of divergence. A woman who has carried a child through a delicate babyhood, or whose attachment to her husband is less sturdy than she expected, often prolongs her mothering unduly: not only at her husband's expense, but to his impatience and, in the end, to some shoulder-shrugging—"Oh, all right, if you want to make a sissy out of him!" Later perhaps, father, making an effort to counteract the sissy deal and "make a man" of him, puts on extra pressure, barks orders, gets angry, banishes the spoiled one to his room. Mother, indignant at such harsh treatment of her darling, slips him a note or a coke and retires in tears to take up the matter with father later.

Unevenness in discipline, whether between two parents or within one parent at different times—indulgent one day, explosive the next—is always confusing to a child and productive of unstable, unbalanced development. When two parents of opposing temperaments or concepts of child rearing start warring, the "softie" gets softer, the "toughie" gets tougher and estrangement sets in.

Today's principle of "child management" is just that. It is "management" which is neither the authoritative "Do it because I say so!" nor the opposite, extreme indulgence. A well "managed" family is one in which there are few laws, few conflicts, few emotional storms. Yet, this does not mean a lawless family, but one that pulls together. During the early years, little children are almost self-operative, pretty well equipped by nature to pursue the route of their own best interests. The parent's job is largely to protect them from doing themselves and others physical harm. They throw and pound, jump and kick because all of this is their workout. They are struggling to get control of their bodily mechanisms. When they are old enough to move about, they begin a new series of workouts, they pull and reach, grasp and clasp and more besides to gain control of their environment. But now the parental interference begins, the "no-no" and "mustn't-mustn't." Instead, there are happy ways of meeting the situations, which will save both household and baby.

Young parents are likely to overtrain the first child from inexperience and lack of acquaintance with accepted methods. Disagreement on these matters between young parents could be avoided if both would refer to Dr. Benjamin Spock's priceless book, *Baby and Child Care*, available at thirty-five cents everywhere in the United States. Incidentally, whether because of the teaching of this little volume, or because of their own intelligence some of the most inexperienced of young parents have joined the ranks of the best and make today a growing army of very well-equipped fathers and mothers.

The Triangle

There seems to be no end to the numbers of men and women who find themselves, wittingly or unwittingly, part of a third dimensional affair, often of a fourth, when two complete married couples are involved. The numbers, themselves, are not so staggering as are the range of persons, nice persons, persons with dignity and standing: young, immature teenagers; neurotic persons who should be in mental hospitals, and, of course, the kind there has always been, the triflers, the opportunists, as well as the plain adventurers.

One has but to attend a few of the national conventions held each year by professional and business groups in the swank hotels of Atlantic City, Miami, or other resorts to know that complete indifference to masculine or feminine charms is a rare "virtue." The resort places are happy hunting grounds, but in most cases, the dip into romance, like the dip into the ocean, is a mere part of the show, fun for a day or two before returning into the groove. Most men and women are taking care of themselves. The men know and the women know who is out for what and act accordingly.

Back at home, there is a large middle range of husbands and wives, restless and unhappy with each other. Wives who fling out threats, "I don't have to stay. I can take care of myself," and husbands who, believing this, feel less guilty when they find themselves shifting their devotion to another.

Coffee breaks at the office, lunch hour, staff dances, picnics and what not, further light romances and beget trivial flirtations, rift or no rift at home, just for the fun of it. But should war really break out and "the boss" arrive pale and distraught, there is bound to be a sympathetic voice, "What's the matter, Dickie dear?" (these first names!) "You look downhearted this morning!" The voice, the question, the little pat on the back don't help the slipping loyalty.

Sometimes, when a wife discovers that a secretary has moved too far into her husband's affections, she will either demand that he send her away or when he is off on a trip arrange to go down to the office to see her. Sending the secretary away has three strikes against it. He doesn't want to lose her; she is a good secretary. He doesn't want to acknowledge "anything" before this office force. He can see her more frequently when she is away from the familiar scene than when in the old surroundings. The visit to the office usually fails. The setting is wrong. The wife is at a disadvantage. She sits in her husband's seat as a usurper, she holds up business and sets the whole place agog.

There is one much more favorable way to meet this situation of a new attraction and that frequently comes through the husband himself. He tries to include his wife in the friendship.

"Mary, you know Deborah. I've spoken of her frequently! Couldn't we ask her out here some night? I'd like you to know her." It is a courageous move and sometimes it helps. Strangely enough, or perhaps not strangely, women who are attracted to the same man often are attracted to each other, sometimes in spite of a known rivalry. For such an association to be carried through successfully, all three must follow the rules. There may be no undercurrents allowed to come to the surface to pass between husband and guest. The wife must free her mind of all speculations and jealousies. "How far has this thing gone!" As for the rival, an invitation into a man's home to meet his wife and family automatically makes known his position to the other in respect to it. From then on the two women have the situation largely in their hands. Overstepping on the girl's part, after this, jealous checking of dates and running through pockets, or calling up on the office phone for no particular business on the wife's part, can put an end to the brave beginning.

SERVICEMEN

Is there anything more that one can say to help the serviceman who returns to find another has taken his place, or the service wife suffering under a similar defection? Men and women who loved each other and were engaged to be married before the draft caught up with them have a good record of faithfulness, married and unmarried. But the girls and boys who were just steadies with no sincere attachment but jumped on the marriage bandwagon partly because "all the others" were jumping and partly for the deeper instinctive feeling of need for survival in some fashion

in the extremity of a war crisis, these young husbands
and wives of the moment have little to build on, and
their divorce record is high.

The most cruel of all situations is the one in which
a serviceman returns home to find his beloved wife
pledged to another, in some instances to a draft
dodger, one of which a young wife preferred, ironi-
cally, to her husband because he was more of a "he-
man!" "I might not have left Tom," she explained later,
"if he had put up a good fight for me."

The alternative to the fighting game is the waiting
game. Often a love affair, whether of a young or a
mature woman, is as insecure as she is herself. It is
made up, like many of the flirtations at the conventions, of a search for adventure, excitement, and a
need for romance. She casts an upward glance, it is
returned, there is a quick, tremulous experience, a few
light, oblique words of love, no words of marriage
and before she realizes it she is seeking a divorce. During the months of waiting something happens to the
romance, the dream becomes less real, the new devotion less devoted, and the admirer slips away. It is
now that a husband can have his say if he wishes to.
A woman's pride will not let her stand alone after a
retreating lover. She can also require that his fences
be mended, too. The question is not only what he can
do to prevent another escape, but what can he do to
make her happy, and what are a few of his own needs?

Can they, too, find happiness together? The inventory-taking will be good for both.

Some women can be kept happy with a family of children, others in presiding over a beautiful home, some in freedom to follow a career or to identify themselves with their husbands' careers. Some men can keep a flirtatious girl happy. Some cannot. An "old sober sides" of a husband of such a woman is destined for grief unless he understands her. But in all cases, masculine rights and possessions must be tempered by vision, the transient affairs held not too seriously and love not permitted to grow chill.

As for the husband, he too requires what most masculine hearts desire, but with less variation than women. A comfortably managed home, a concern for his business interests, a handful of congenial friends whom they may invite to dinner or an evening with men for golf or cards, or bowling, and a word with a pretty girl if she drops by. After the central, fundamental bulk of a man's interests and labors are given over to his family, the "fringe benefits" of his life, his recreation, his leisure hours, his special pursuits, should be his own. Husbands must be free, neither housebound, nor wifebound nor childrenbound if spontaneous and happy companionship is to endure. It is when freedom has *not* survived that it is sought through illegitimate affairs. Separation and divorce are harsh instruments.

Unsuspected Pitfalls

With mental illness increasing alarmingly, it is not surprising to find, even in highly organized working groups, a fair number of emotionally disturbed persons. Yet, often strongly talented, they accomplish their work with considerable skill, draw their salaries, and, not infrequently, marry.

These highly intelligent persons, both men and women, are sometimes distinctly charming and others are naturally attracted to them, as an old friend of mine was a few years ago. Soon after the honeymoon his bride became a chronic invalid, would have nothing to do with love or money, for either love or money. The husband carried on alone, made all purchases, paid all bills. After years he died of heart failure very suddenly. Overnight the invalid wife became well, assumed the care of the household. Basket on her arm, money in her purse, she sallied forth to market. No husband, no sex; all was well.

Not so frequently, the emotional disturbance lies in the husband who, because he is the breadwinner, cannot so readily, or so completely surrender. Yet men develop all kinds of illnesses—ulcers, phobias, migraines—and indulge in all sorts of bizarre hobbies and occupations in their efforts at release from tension. One of these men has invented during his marriage some five hundred or more gadgets with drawings and models complete. Yet not one of them has ever been patented and placed on the market to give encouragement to further efforts. What would you call this, a hobby or a phobia? Oddly enough, the personal relationships of these wavering and ill-prepared people—ill-prepared to meet life's realities—tend to remain strong and steady toward each other. They stay together in surprising numbers. But then, husbands and wives tend to stick by their dependent mates, who hold them with a sincere and childlike affection.

When there is no bond, when, in spite of dependence, the disturbed partner turns against his (or her) mate—endurance is not the word. Endurance only postpones the day of medical help and lessens its favorable outcome. Yet any suggestion of professional care to a disturbed person usually meets with resistance. "There's nothing the matter with me! I'm all right!" Sometimes a son or daughter, even fairly young children are more successful in their persuasion of father or mother than a wife or husband toward whom hostilities have been directed. These efforts failing, there are two more to choose between, according to the severity of the emotional status of the partner; to leave her (or him) in charge of her own family, parents or grown children, or to consult with her physician, asking him to take charge and use his own medical judgment in appraising the whole situation. Two things are sure, the disturbed mind is not one to guide its own recovery and not to provide for its recovery is negligence.

But again, family members will say, "Mary is not really a mental case. She is just 'different,' even perhaps difficult at times." Different, difficult, neurotic, psychopathic persons, whatever the term, may be outwardly even as you or I—economically productive, earning their salaries, keeping up their homes, caring for their children, but, even so, the future is unknown and the present is the time for treatment.

Difficult, even disloyal as the departure of husband or wife may be for a conscientious mate, the shock of separation often has a stimulating and even beneficial effect. Yet, whether it does or does not, when marriage has lost all that it holds, or gives promise of ever holding, and has become an empty shell, it is infinitely better to bring it to a close.

The last sort of person who steps in to tangle up her own love affairs and those of others is that anomalous person who drifts about town with little known background, little known knowledge of her social status. Has she a husband anywhere? Is she divorced? Who is her family? Nobody seems to know, yet she has lots of followers, men and women who fill her leisure moments without too much close questioning.

Recently, one of these gay entertaining women caught the eye of a young happy-go-lucky man at a company dance, just as she became aware of him. In a moment, introductions were effected and the two were out on the dance floor, cheek to cheek. Later by an hour or two, the girl's escort sought out her new friend.

"I've had an unexpected telephone call and must leave. Could you take care of my date?"

On the way home the girl suggested they stop for coffee. Later, at her home, she invited him in for drinks and to meet her mother. The neighborhood, the home, the mother were totally beyond the expectations of the most imaginative. Luxury, good taste, culture prevailed in every detail. Conversation was delightful. At leaving, the new guest was warmly invited to return. Flattered, curious, rather than attracted, he responded, "How about dinner with me tomorrow night?"

For the next week or two dinners or luncheons together followed every day. With the weekend came an invitation from the girl's mother to spend it with them at their cottage in the mountains. Unexpectedly, the mother was not able to leave and the two went on alone. While at the cottage, there was little or no lovemaking. The young hostess showed her guest into a room, removed from hers. But, on Sunday morning, over the coffee, she asked suddenly, almost blithely, "Would I make a good wife?"

"You couldn't make me a good wife, because I have one," her guest replied.

"Could I make anyone a good wife?" she persisted.

Something beneath the surface, something in the intensity of the girl's voice made this happy-go-lucky man of easy morals stop and think. At last he said,

"Girl, you have everything, but one. Do you know what that is?"

Yes, she knew. She knew it was warmth. Warmth of the sort that opens a woman's arms to the man she loves and closes them around him. But she did not have it to give. This unhappy, restless, man-questing woman is just one of thousands, some of whom are ready to marry any man for purposes of their own, some who are hoping to beguile or pique an erring husband, some who never have achieved marriage and are nursing a suffering ego, some who want to marry on their own terms.

Others suffer sexual difficulties; they are frigid like the beautiful, cultured girl of our story, or they are highly sexed (nymphomaniacs), or they demand a variety in their love objects—dark men, light men, young men. One may pursue the aesthetic male, like the monks of old, another may be seeking a roué, a libertine—all of them, products of their own history of growth, training, and experience, are constantly planning, working, striving toward fulfillment and tranquility within. The sophisticated man, married or unmarried, is able to appraise these women or intuitively to keep aloof and free from them. But the unsophisticated, the impressionable or rejected man is often caught to his grief, sometimes even to his undoing.

A third person who comes into the life of a man and his wife is not necessarily a disruptive force. If their union is secure and happy, bound by ties of love, home, and strength of family, no third person can weaken it. But, if the marriage is already declining, whether acknowledged or unacknowledged, a third person, if just "the right person," can threaten a whirlwind. Threaten!

Always, skeptics contend that in matters of romance, as in matters of business, every man has his price. Yet the experts know that for every husband and wife who separate, more remain together even in spite of the pull of an outside interest. Such interest may or may not be the whirlwind that brings destruction, it can be no more than an interlude—a brief rapturous throwback to youth—or it may bring a sharp awakening, a recasting and evaluation of the years behind and the years ahead. With any chance at all for the reclamation of the old bond, most men and women will try their best to save a failing marriage, but when every effort has been made and every effort has failed, each individual life must not fail with it. Each must live his own life out to its completion.

Immaturity and haste, it seems to me, are the two great offenders in today's unsuccessful marriages, the two that bring them to an early close.

Chapter XI

The Outer Circle

WHEN it comes to family circles and their boundaries, how far out is "outer" and how far in is "inner"? I am prompted to say, "Look at your sugar bowls." There are two in my dining room. The large one belonged to my mother's tea service and held easily two pounds of sugar for her family table. The other, which has served my little family quite adequately, holds but a few ounces. Sleeping rooms follow sugar bowls. There are enough for the immediate family but an old-fashioned guest room ready and waiting is a luxury most of us do not possess. Is the boundary question answered? Father, mother, and children are inner. Grandparents, uncles, aunts, and cousins are outer, but they are still family, though a trifle dethroned and with them have gone many intangibles and invaluables but not, we hope, irretrievables.

More arresting witnesses of the one-generation family can be seen any day at a cash and carry market where a grandfather or grandmother, an unattached aunt or uncle stands in line with his little pushcart at the checker's desk. It is not difficult to recognize them with their thimbleful of supplies, their three tomatoes, six apples, a half pound of butter, a quart or two of milk, twelve potatoes. You know they are returning to their little single apartments or to the old, now empty home where each still remains like a lonely leaf on some ancestral tree.

The trend toward this one-generation family is upon us, but it is not yet a fully accomplished fact. A European-born friend has two grandparents in her home, one over eighty, the other over ninety—her own mother and her husband's. Europeans have a greater parental fidelity than we in America have today, a more tenacious hold on old customs. In contrast, another friend, and her mother and her mother's sister—all three of them widows—live separately and apparently contentedly alone.

One wonders whether in reducing the old three- and four-generation family we are not depriving our children of much that they need for their own progress and development. And would not, perhaps, the individual freedom sought for in the one-generation family have been more lastingly sustained if the home arena had been kept a little more diverse, if the family culture had been representative of a greater span of years and a wider variety of interests? After all, these differences have their value and are eventually to be met outside, if not inside, one's home. The narrowing down of a family is, it seems to me, a kind of escapism from adaptability, a fear of conformity from which, in the end, no one does escape.

In addition, there is the more tangible loss of the contribution these same relatives can make during these days of the younger wives' and mothers' entrance and adoption into the ranks of the employed. Not for many a year has there been a time when a household had greater need of a truly devoted parent-substitute than it has now when father and mother in pursuit of business are yet concerned for the welfare of their children.

A generation ago, a household did not come to a dead stop when the mother of the family left for the day. There was always a grandmother, or a maiden aunt, or a widowed cousin to take up the reins and carry on. Between times they helped with the housework, kept the family mending basket from overflowing, read stories at bedtime, heard lessons, were, in short, auxiliary parents for mothers in heavily populated families. "Aunt Mary, will you sew up this rip in my coat?" "Grandmother, are my new mittens almost ready?"

A summer or two ago I visited a household like this. A whole wardrobe of dresses was flung over grandmother's bed all to be altered before three or four granddaughters left for college. Significantly, this grandmother lived in a little home of her own, a stone's throw from her daughter's home, but the life of the two households was closely knit. Meals were impartially shared, refrigerators impartially raided by the children, and beds in both houses impartially occupied. Of the two homes, grandmother's was the livelier. One of this kind of grandmother, so dear to the hearts of children, boasts of her greatest compliment. Fresh from the sand-lot her brood came dashing in one afternoon for refreshment, popped their heads in at her door, coke bottles in hand, and said, "Gram, why don't you come out and play ball with us, we'll let you be pitcher!"

But over the nation, the grandmothers and Aunt Marys are for the most part living their own lives, filling their time and their purses with independent jobs. You find them in department stores behind the counters, or serving in eating places, or assisting in libraries or hospitals, and you find them building up a new profession as "sitters" (strictly a misnomer) in caring for other people's children.

Let anyone who feels censure or is sensitive about the segregation of these generations realize that it has its long-established precedent. Down in the mountains of Kentucky where change takes place slowly, and there are no department stores or eating places to give grandmothers and aunts employment, there is a traditional custom which dramatically puts them in second place without question. When the time comes for a son to bring home a wife, the old home-place is set in order and, upon arrival of the young couple, father and mother, dressed in their best—looking, I imagine, very much like Grant Wood's "American Gothic"— step outside the front door. There they stand on either side of it, not to fling their arms around the newcomers and lead them in, but to stand without while they pass in and take possession of the old home-place, its new master and mistress. What happens to the parents? They follow, deposed, because there is no place else for them to go.

Our kinder, modern custom leaves father and mother in possession of their home while the young people take themselves off happily to establish a home-place of their own. Like children off to camp they sing in parody:

> "No more parents, no more don'ts,
> No more I wills and I won'ts."

Then follows for both generations a season of learning to know each other. In addition to the many personal adjustments that young husbands and wives must make between themselves, there are the new parents-in-law! Automatically and inevitably burlesqued, the in-law situation is thrust upon them:

> "How do you like your 'in-laws'?"
> "Are you going to live with your 'in-laws'?"
> "What are you going to call your 'in-laws'?"

Nobody uses names or recognizes parental relationships. Bill's or Sally's mother and father by marriage are just bogies, somethings less than human about which they must be fortified to defend themselves.

Chief assistance comes from the jokesmith of comic sections in Sunday supplements, radio, television, and burlesque shows with a mother-in-law the chief target. Even religious groups try to quicken their programs and draw a laugh at her expense. In one such program recently the speaker said, "Divine love is so great it can level mountains, yes, it can even help you lose your hate and learn to love your mother-in-law!" Radio announcers who must be careful of blackmail in attacking individuals have no inhibitions in slaying all mothers of sons and daughters. An announcer of a high-class automobile finished his commercial by proclaiming, "You'll even be willing to invite your mother-in-law for a drive in it." Another commercial for a breakfast food promised, "it'll make you so strong you can even stand up to your mother-in-law!"

So many have been the difficulties arising between young couples and their new parents by marriage, due in large measure to these built-in and usually groundless fears, that family relationships have become the *Number One* marriage issue. Not finances, not working wives, not children or recreation, but the newly acquired family of adults is the present active concern of young married couples, as well as those not so young. No matter how much young people love each other, they love their parents too and are not happy over the prospect of unaccustomed unfriendliness and disruption between them. If there is any way to meet this situation by looking at it impersonally and reasonbly let us do it now, they say, before anyone gets hurt!

To make this mutual aid possible, several guides may serve:

1. Discount the mother-in-law and stepmother jokes. They are as unfounded as many other gags made to draw a laugh without regard to any far-reaching and damaging effects.

2. Forget the term "in-laws," remember that it applies to your mate's own father and mother. There is no "in-lawish" quality in that relationship. It is a natural, deep, and lifelong bond.

3. Give everybody a chance before judgments are made. During the first year of marriage everyone is on probation and no one does himself justice.

4. If your mate is the finest in all the world, remember who is largely responsible. Good parents make good in-laws. Happy families make happy families.

5. Don't ask your new parents-in-law to defend themselves. In our courts a person is considered innocent until he is proven guilty.

6. Last of all, let efforts at friendship be reciprocal. Love begets love, and knowledge dispels intolerance.

TROUBLE SPOTS

The word that one hears most frequently among young marrieds is "interference." "Why do they want to interfere with us?" "Why can't they let us lead our own lives?" Around this "interference" most other irritations circle and lead, not too infrequently, to separation and divorce. "She's either my wife or she's their daughter," one irate husband declared. "And I don't mean maybe."

Desire for self-government, independence, freedom from parental control on the part of young people is the factor most frequently involved. Young people want personal and collective emancipation and they want it complete. Through their marriage they have publicly and legally stepped out of childhood into an adult state. The branch has been severed from the parent tree. The setting up of a home together by a young husband and wife is another visible demonstration of this achievement and they don't want it lessened by parents. It is their party and they want it left to them just as they did in their early teens when they danced in the living room with lights out and demanded that no grownups be at hand to supervise. Later, after a few years when the first flush of freedom has been savored—and not sabotaged—the guards are lightened a bit and the "No Admittance" sign taken down.

The reverse is true of the parents. During those

first years when two young people are insisting upon living their own life, their parents are feeling their loss from the home most keenly. A sudden break makes it all the harder. The house is empty. "It's like a tomb in here," says father, after the last wedding presents have been moved out. "I wonder what they're doing tonight," mother says, and suggests that they drive over and see. In the end they both go window-shopping. Every chair, every table, every teapot is as though marked with the children's names. "Do you think we could send that breakfast set out on approval?" mother asks father, trying to keep off forbidden ground, trying, too, to ease the pain of loneliness.

You see how it is. The young people need and want a clean-cut break, the parents need and want a gradual one. By the time the children are ready to stand a little bit of parent again, the parents are becoming accustomed to the absence of their children. It seems to me there should be a compromise and, if each generation could understand the position of the other as natural and universal with no personal undercurrents or overtones, the whole matter could be worked out, with, as the student said, "No feelings hurt."

To this end I have jotted down a few of the chief points of concern that young people have voiced most frequently. They should serve at least as a guide toward a more harmonious and happy unity between parents, parents-in-law, and their children during the trying first years of marriage.

Frequent Questions Asked by Young People

I.   Is it always a mistake to live with one's parents after marriage?

II. Shall parents seek to influence a son's or a daughter's marriage choice?

III. In general, should parents give opinions and advice to their married children, unasked?

IV. To get started shall young couples accept loans from their parents?

V.   Must one have regular visiting and letter-writing days?

VI. How does one address the new parents-in-law?

VII. Is it always best to have a relative as a sitter for the children?

I. *Is it always a mistake to live with one's parents after marriage?*

Not always, but usually. Everyday experience and observation, as well as the results of formal surveys discourage "doubling up" unless it is necessary, and when it is necessary, and not a matter of choice, it is more difficult than ever. A great many girls who married G. I.'s just before they left for camp or service, remained with their parents rather than attempting to live alone. Parents of other young people, especially those who are still in school, have converted third floors or garages into housekeeping apartments, have built additions on spare corners, or have erected little guest houses in the rear of their own houses. Such temporary accommodations make marriage possible many times, but they should have no strings attached and everyone should be free as air. Stone walls may not a prison make but parental quarters may, if that is not where one wants to be and freedom is curtailed.

One such situation came to light recently. The very young husband—he looked about nineteen—was attending college and working heavy hours out of school to supplement his G. I. subsidy. The young wife was working, too, in another town where both were making their home with the young teen-age wife's parents. The several hours a day that the boy needed for study were spent driving back and forth between towns. Health, grades, spirits suffered. Why didn't they close the gap? Obviously the little wife should have joined her student-husband. Everyone can guess the answer: an underaged daughter who had been given parental consent to marry, if she would remain at home. Either the girl must be released from her promise or the husband must leave school if they are to remain together.

II. *Shall parents seek to influence a son's or a daughter's marriage choice?*

No, and they rarely do. Most of them do not have the opportunity, for the children are frequently away at college or elsewhere. If they happen to live in the same town, it is natural for a son to wish his parents to meet the girl who may be their future daughter-in-law. And of course, she would be happy to meet and know them. A friendship established before marriage would do much to prevent some of the misunderstandings that occur when two women, totally unknown to each other, meet to share for the rest of their lives the love and devotion of one man—son and husband.

A daughter's husband, in contrast, usually has been a familiar figure in a family long before he becomes a member of it. Mutual likes and dislikes, general opinions of each other have long been established. "Duncan is one of us already," mother will say and hopes that there will be no change. Yet if daughter's favorite man does not find favor with her family "for just cause," the family should have the privilege of any outsider to respond to the marriage ritual's opportunity "to speak now or forever hold his peace." The difference is that family objections are to be made before the ceremony, and in private.

Most parents have their children's welfare and happiness at heart and rarely would they question their choice for personal or selfish reasons. Whether a son or daughter were influenced by their adverse opinion, should it be given, would depend largely upon two things: the depth of his attachment for the one he loves, and his entire childhood relationship to his parents.

A young man or woman who has been permitted to

grow up in freedom, to form his own friendships, and to act upon his own judgment as he grows will listen on those rare occasions when his parents do offer an opinion, especially on such a serious matter as a prospective wife or husband. Once the subject is considered, it is left and no matter what the decision, welcome is ready for their child's own marriage choice. It must in the end be a son's or a daughter's own choice. It can never be a parent's choice or anybody's else.

III. *In general, should parents give opinions and advice to their married children, unasked?*

I know many who don't because they know or feel that it might be unwelcome. "I wait until I'm asked," they say. "I don't want to interfere!" That word again! Think a minute. Do young people themselves, their friends, neighbors, people in general, ever give opinions to young marrieds, unasked? You know they do!—opinions all the way from how to paint their own furniture to how to patch up their first quarrel.

Giving advice or opinions is a human frailty. On the other hand, those same opinions, asked or unasked, sound or unsound, have value, not only as an expression of friendship and interest, but as a starting point for many original ideas. People who lecture or write are seldom without notebook and pencil, not to quote or adopt another's ideas or even to preserve them, but to use them as a starting point for new trains of thought of their own. It doesn't seem quite fair, does it, to deny parents the liberty of free speech which belongs to everyone else?

Whether one acts upon their opinions or follows their advice is another matter and depends upon how well they are equipped to speak. Neither age nor youth gives value to an opinion unless it is well founded. But when it is, it should have a hearing. Not long ago I saw a former clergyman sitting silent in his son's living room during a discussion on religion. In another home his would have been the first and the last word spoken. I was reminded of a little girl who would not accept her skilled accountant-father's figuring on her arithmetic problem because he didn't do it like the teacher.

But in justice to those who are irked by the opinion of their parents even when it is authoritative and professional, one must admit it is only a self-protective, schizophrenic rejection. They proudly recommend their parents to others, for it is not so much the ideas that they run from as it is the possible cost to their independence. They are afraid of some parental leftover fragment of coercion that might accompany the opinion or advice (if it were advice). Any voluntary expression from outsiders is quite another matter. It can be taken or left with no feelings hurt, with no sense of enforced obligation.

Because of the frequency of the question in regard

to accepting parental opinion, one would almost conclude that all young people were resistant to parental counsel. Nothing is "all," but the trend is active and it is strong. How strong it is depends, as we mentioned earlier, on the two generations themselves, the parents and the children they reared.

Fathers and mothers who belong to the old school of "Thou shalt nots" or "While you are in my house you do as I say" or "It doesn't matter what other people do" have built up so much inner resistance to authority that their children in adult years have no will for any more whether from their own parents or from their parents-in-law. Children by marriage, without ties of love and affection or even knowledge of their new parents, are even more resistant to the thought of authority after a childhood surfeited by it. You cannot blame them. They would run away from the Angel Gabriel himself, and reject him if he were presented as a future father-in-law.

Thanks to the rapid growth of family life education, mental hygiene, and personal relationships now increasingly available as studies in schools and colleges, there is a growing understanding between the two generations. Parents are less autocratic, young people freer to plan and execute their own lives and therefore less frequently ready to do battle for their rights. From this new easement in childhood, everyone will benefit: students will be less derisive of their instructors, employees less inclined to shift blame to others, young teachers less resistive to supervisors' or principals' suggestions, and, yes, daughters-in-law and sons-in-law less on the defensive toward their new parents. Where home rule during the growing up years has been reasonable and understanding, there will be little inclination to fear any "in-law" rule after marriage. The accustomed mantle will fall on everyone, the parent image will remain largely the same.

IV. *To get started shall young couples accept loans from their parents?*

Business loans are better than personal loans if there is adequate collateral. Often there is none, and then loans from parents become an individual decision. If two young people would rather be "penny paupers and proud of it," as many of them declare, rather than borrow from their parents, they should be permitted to, for any assistance that creates a feeling of obligation or indebtedness on either side would be a mistake. Rarely does a true father or mother give financial aid to either son or daughter with thought of personal advantage or profit of any sort. What they do for their children they do for love because they belong to them, married or unmarried, and always will.

Yet many generous and devoted parents ask for notes to be signed for the records and in justice to their other sons and daughters, who have not received aid during the parents' lifetime. Other parents keep no records at all and expect no repayment, deciding each situation on its own merits. The economic value of a college degree to one child is offset by financial aid to another. Parents weigh these values, and in the end they are usually just.

It is not always a son's or a daughter's own parent who comes to his rescue in time of need. Frequently it is the parent-in-law who is even more generous than an "own" parent. Said a young husband humorously when asked how he liked his mother-in-law, "I like her fine, she can always be relied upon to stay with the kids and pull me out of debt."

V. *Must one have regular visiting and letter-writing days?*

Said one young husband, "I don't like to be pinned down." He is right, nobody likes to be regimented from week to week to visit anybody, not even his own family. But there is also truth in the saying, "What you don't do every day (or week, or month) you soon don't do any day," and it applies perfectly to letters and visits to relatives.

"I get tired," another young husband said, "of never having a Sunday alone with my own family. One Sunday my parents come to dinner with us and the next we go to their house. The third Sunday my father-in-law and mother-in-law come to our house and the fourth we go to theirs. I am about ready to leave town." The remedy, of course, for this sort of tread-mill is not to have started it. Few routine affairs retain their zest after a short time. And as young people enlarge their social horizons, they do not like to be bound by any set arrangements. I recall a young mother years ago who scandalized her circle of friends by saying she was not going to become a slave to any domestic routine, not even her husband's meals and her babies' feedings!

As for the letters, they too should be kept free of routine. The standard schedule (if there is a standard) is once a day for lovers, once a week for wives, and once a month for mothers. Parents who are aware of the pressure of work and the demands of school, church, and community on their heads-of-family sons and daughters, do not complain about belated letters, hope only that the hours gained are spent in rest, recreation, and sleep. In large families the "round robin" letter is a timesaver. It starts with mother and father, is read by each child in turn as it comes along, receives his contribution and is sent on its way. In the end it comes back to its source bringing fresh news of all the children.

VI. *How does one address the new parents-in-law?*

That would depend, it seems to me, on the age, the general approachability of the new parents-in-law, and how much one liked them. In this day of first names when titles of all sorts have been discarded from chief justices and presidents on down the line, I should think plain everyday parents-in-law would be willing to settle for a mere Jane or Jack, Tom or Ann. If there is any hesitancy about first names, one can always make up an appropriate but friendly nickname to ease formality, or if worst comes to worst, wait for the babies to arrive and adopt their names, "Nannie," "Grammie," or whatever. It all depends on the individual.

VII. *Is it always best to have a relative as a sitter for the children?*

Not always, but usually. Most grandparents and aunts, especially maiden aunts with no children of their own, are devoted to those closely related to them. The children themselves feel a bond, warm to them in a fashion not accorded to the run-of-the-mill sitter. So far as their well-being is concerned, psychologically and physically, some member of the family is far and away the best of all parent substitutes. "Let's have Aunt Ellen stay with us always!"

But these days, when families have become scattered, relatives are not always available. Those near at hand have found steady employment which they can't afford to give up, and may not wish to. Yet there are many elderly women in our families, physically unable to take exacting commercial positions, who are adequately fitted to be homekeepers for their daughters and sisters, and caretakers of their children.

To these women one would not be able to offer an hourly return for their services as one would to a stranger, but if they were not too well-secured financially, one could send a monthly stipend to their banks just as one would to any member of the family "who could use it." But everyone recognizes that whatever is given in acknowledgment to a grandmother or aunt who goes into a household to take charge—if she does take charge and is not just a figurehead—can never be adequately rewarded in terms of financial gain. Her fullest reward comes to her in the feeling of belonging and the devotion of the children.

However, there is one hazard which might lose her both the children and her position as their second mother: the differences in home and child management which are conspicuous between women of two generations. Yet there need be no conflict if both will settle for the standards of child specialist and not try to work it out by themselves. Yet even such godsends as Dr. Spock and Dr. Gesell who put to rout most varying opinions on child care, need at times to be cut down and fitted to size.

However, if by chance older family members in charge are not open to change in the interest of general conformity to modern standards of conduct and child management, the welfare of the children would determine the success or continuance of the arrangement. Little children who are in the midst of learning their first lessons in socialization—toilet habits, eating, sleeping, adapting to other children—must not be confused by conflicting ideas. They must have uniformity. But older children of school age are matured by variation and need to learn to adapt to different people and different ways.

The degree of an older child's acceptance of another person's "say so" rests largely with the two women, the mother and the mother substitute. Mother is the pacemaker. From the children's first year she has stood for the whole world outside. Her word is unquestioned. It takes precedence over all others. Yet everyone knows each family's yardstick is not a universal one, every household has its own. Mother's obligation to grandmother or to any other person who comes in to take her place is to support her, not expecting her to be a mouthpiece—"Mother wants you to do this," "Mother wants you to do that"—but a representative to whom she has passed on her authority, her scepter of government, to reign in her absence.

Grandmother has obligations too. She must be very sure that, in keeping her own personality intact, she does nothing to weaken or destroy the children's confidence in their mother. Mother is still mother and there must be no usurping of her affections or authority. One grandmother who came to keep house for her daughter dismayed her by setting the table in such a fashion that she presided as head of the family and subordinated her daughter to a seat at the side with the children. Such a shifting of position may not be intentional, but is open to question. Grandmother is queen in her own home, but when she steps into her daughter's home even to take charge, her daughter is still the head of the family. Conflict over this situation should not arise if the welfare of the children is of mutual concern.

These elderly parents may have their apartments, their hotel rooms, may boast of their independence, but let no one be deceived. No older woman cherishes independence over association with her children. The new place for her in the family, which the employment of her daughter or daughter-in-law makes possible, should be of the greatest comfort to both generations and will be if they can get together on essentials—if, that is, grandmother is able to feel herself as a contemporary, not as a discard, or, as she would say, "a back number." And if she, herself, is able to *be* a contemporary through her understanding of modern thought and ways, she will be accepted as such. Both parents and children of two or three generations have one lesson to learn: years do not separate, but ideas do. These must be in harmony if mother and grandmother are to share in the management of one household.

STEPPARENTS

A second most discouraging situation in the family circle is that of stepfather and stepmother. As with the parents-in-law, the jokesmith has been there beforehand and they enter upon a relationship which is all but wrecked for them before they start.

THE STEPFATHER

Stepfathers, like fathers-in-law, have a less arduous assignment than stepmothers because they are largely removed from the domestic scene. They leave the management of the younger children to their mother but the teen-agers give them plenty of grief once they start to lend a hand. A typical attitude was expressed in a bull session by one of several neighborhood boys. "I've got two dads, both strict. One I listen to—that's my own dad. He's gone now. The other—the new one— he can just whistle." The difficulties of stepfathers, and this applies to adopting fathers as well, are caused, usually, by a too-sudden taking over of the disciplinary side of the parental rôle, which, after all, is theirs only by virtue of circumstance. "You're not my father," the young children say, and the older ones act it.

A stepfather tells me he has two ulcers, one for each stepson. They run him ragged. The family has two cars. One he has to keep in a downtown garage in order to get to work in the morning. He takes two newspapers and a half dozen magazines which he spends an hour or more looking for when he comes home at night. The radio, the television, and numerous other "noisemakers" fill the air constantly with no time out. Something, it seems to me, is the matter with their mother. Either she never had control of her sons or she did not make adequate preparation for their new father and his part in the new family setup.

A widow or a divorcee with children, who remarries, has two obligations that she does not have when she marries for the first time. A young woman over eighteen may marry without the consent of her parents, but a widow should think twice before she marries without the approval of her children. They must have become friends with the prospective father and the liking should be reciprocal. A man may say to his fiancée, "I want to be a good father to your children," but that does not mean that they will let him be what he considers a good father to be. Their acceptance of him cannot be taken for granted. They must be won over gradually, genuinely, not by gifts or outward display of interest or "playing up" to them, but by those personal attributes children are quick to recognize—honesty, sincerity, and friendliness—a winning over which must be accomplished not after, but before the wedding that resentment at an interloper may be forestalled. Much of the friction that arises between stepparents and their new children is like the friction between parents-in-law and their new children when they come into an intimate relationship, as strangers, before they have won their way.

The alternative is the prospective father who says, "You mustn't think that I am going to interfere with the management of your children. I have had no experience and they wouldn't like it anyway." Though this father shows more understanding of children than he claims, he still misses it. No one can become an integral part of any family and remain detached from it. It is not to be accepted and it is all but impossible to achieve. Participation is the keynote in family life as it is in all business, civic, or church life. Exclusion from the children's affairs would soon bring about more exclusion of mother from his own affairs and he would be left feeling out of it. In the end he would take himself off in one way or another, probably with another girl who had no children. The same thing that brings about rapport and understanding between new parents-in-law and their children is also necessary to bring about acceptance between stepchildren and their new parents. It is daily personal association which promotes liking, confidence, and friendship. And this must be established emphatically before any attempts at discipline, guidance, or even critical comments are undertaken. When acceptance is established then authority may follow but not until.

Stepchildren not only resent a new father's early assumption of control, but they resent him partly from loyalty to their own father and partly from personality reasons. As one girl expressed it, "If Mom was going to marry anyone, why didn't she marry somebody else!" Then there is the not infrequent new husband who moves into the home of his new wife with all his effects, which disturbs them no end. "Where does he think he can put all this stuff of his?" As time goes on and mother continues paying the taxes, the house repairs, the upkeep of all sorts, continues her employment at the office, meets the grocery and milk bills, signs the contract for a new car—"We need two now" —not friendliness but hostility is bound to awaken. "What goes on here?" the children ask.

The later marriage of a mother, whether widowed or divorced, offers a number of financial considerations. Unless the new husband has planned to adopt the children and finance their rearing and education, women may not take these measures for granted. Most of all she must be sure that any marriage of hers does not deplete the children's share of their father's estate and provision for them, whether legally secured or not. The unattached woman with money—any money at all—is a ready mark for a self-seeking, money-seeking male. Many of them, widowed or divorced with scant or uncertain income, are quick to take on another wife and her children if an ample or even supplementary income is available through her. On their part, women are only too ready to fill the vacancy and relieve the loneliness of a manless existence. Recently a woman who had divorced the father of her three girls for gambling and nonsupport, much to their disgust married immediately a successor with the same failings. "He'll take all Mom's got and then she'll throw him out and marry another just like him. Where do we come in?" But you wouldn't think with three daughters that this woman would need another person to take care of. No, a stepfather cannot expect to have the slightest prestige with his wife's children if he accepts so much as one dollar of her money.

When the opposite takes place, when the new father has a home of his own with the means to support their mother which will permit her to give up her own employment and allow them all to live comfortably in his home, then the relationship moves along more smoothly. This man has recognized rights. He is on his own ground. Children are quick to appreciate these things. In any case where the new parent has earned his welcome into the family and has been accepted in very truth, mother must be ready to do her part in his gradual assumption of the father rôle. She must have created an attitude of support which the children catch and respond to. First of all, she must come to a definite decision in her own mind in regard to her husband's relationship to her children which will dispel all fears. Sitting on the edge of her chair worrying, fearful that somebody will say something to annoy him or begging the children "to do it anyway," just to keep the peace and she'll make it up to them later, trying, that is, to be a buffer between her children and their stepfather, all of this is merely dodging the issue and leaving the children without the guidance and security that they ought to find in him.

There is another thought about stepchildren in relation to their parents who remarry. Children are monogamous in their feeling. To them, marriage is a continuous state reaching back into the unknown and carrying forward into all time. Mom and dad belong to each other, and they, the children, belong to them. Separation, divorce comes as a shock, a disruption, and a genuine tragedy in their lives. It is this feeling of children and their grief at the thought of the separation of their parents which has held and does hold innumerable homes together. Small wonder that remarriage, the replacement of mother or father by a stranger cannot be welcomed by most children. He is a usurper, an intruder, everything which loyalty forbids. Small wonder again that stepfathers ever succeed and when they do they must have achieved through a long and careful campaign of friendship.

THE STEPMOTHER

The stepmother's winning a family of children is both easier and more difficult than that of a stepfather. She gains or loses more quickly, more factors are involved, including the age-old handicap of the jokesmith and fairy tales from Cinderella on down. Truthfully, stepmothers, like mothers-in-law, are forced to get off to a bad start. Yet the world is full of women who have overcome their handicaps and their husbands and children have risen up to call them blessed. If she has children of her own she will say, "I know no difference, they are all mine."

When a stepmother comes into a motherless home of very young children, she is likely to be welcomed as a nurse is welcomed by a suffering patient. The comforting mother-touch has been missed, the home has not felt like home. The children are happy to feel someone again in charge and recognize her right to organize and direct them. It would be an untactful, unsympathetic woman who could not win a houseful of very young children if she wished to. But like the stepfather, she must not move too swiftly with the older children, make drastic changes, become authoritative or "bossy." Certainly, not by word or look criticize the departed mother.

In the case of divorce, no matter how a child himself feels about the mother who caused the family disruption, he will not welcome the judgment of anybody else. A stepmother who found her stepson tight-lipped not only toward her but toward his father tried to come to the rescue by showing how justified his father was in asking for a divorce. The boy left home and refused to return. It happens. A stepparent does well to avoid references to a divorced parent unless the children speak up first.

The same is true in relation to the father. Many

times a marriage has broken up because of some specific trait, say alcoholism, when all the qualities that attracted a man to his wife in the first place still remain. Those he still loves and admires, those make it difficult for him to talk to anyone who might not understand. As for the children, they are entitled to some satisfying explanation of their parents' separation which should be given by the father himself, or, should it be a case in which the children are left with the mother, by her. Honor demands that explanations be fair and impartial, difficult as that may be. Often a divorce has no specific reason or none that can be revealed to a child, such as infidelity. More often it is a personal, untranslatable, nebulous something which the courts call "incompatibility." "We just didn't get along together," one says to the children and as they grow older they will come to understand.

The situation is quite different when a beloved mother has died. She should be happily, actively remembered in the home she has established, and this the new mother can promote with grace and acceptability.

If becoming a stepmother to a family of half-grown children is a courageous affair, adding a new baby might seem a greater one. But it can be a miraculously unifying experience. Children love babies. A baby born to their father, bearing their name, brought from the hospital to their home is *their* baby!

Should there have been any lack of warmth in the

new mother's welcome into the family, it will disappear now as she draws the whole family into the aura surrounding the little new brother or sister. This, not so much by words as by tuning in upon the children's feelings and carrying along with them. Interesting observations have been made in regard to the later relationship of these half-brothers and sisters. Often there is a feeling of full brotherhood and sisterhood. The "step," the "half" is forgotten. It is "My brother Jack," or "My sister Susan." When the "step" is omitted in speaking of the mother then there has been at last a much-desired achievement and all in the family "belong" equally.

THE UNMARRIEDS

We cannot close this chapter on the members of the second-string team in family life without a word for those devoted uncles and aunts whom the world calls bachelors and spinsters. Nobody who has not had a bachelor uncle or a maiden aunt can know how much they add to the completeness of the family circle, even though their own lives are judged incomplete by biological standards. Why these nice people have never married is always something of a mystery, and why they don't, is another. But as the years accumulate, the bachelors seem to accept their, shall I say, plight or fate? whereas the ladies, the spinsters, are of another mind. They are still hoping. Parenthetically, I have never known a woman who thought she was not young enough or attractive enough to marry and have known but one who said she had never regretted being unwed.

People often comfort unmarried women with the platitude, "You could not have accomplished so much in your profession if you had had domestic obligations." The answer comes, one should always accomplish more because of the added support, inspiration, and encouragement a happy marriage brings. As for the older spinster and her hopes, a friends tells me of the recent marriage of her father, a cultured gentleman of eighty-nine, to a maiden of eighty-three. The daughter, feeling the age of the bride and groom might be a matter of too much comment in their small town, suggested a private ceremony and no extensive press notices. But she did not know her unclaimed virgin. When you have suffered the despised state of spinsterhood all of your eighty-three years (almost), stepping into marriage requires all the fanfare that is every bride's due.

As for the bachelor and his bachelorhood, that is an entirely different matter. His is the privilege of choice as the maiden's is not. Presumably he remains single because he wants to, though why he wants to, or, perhaps better expressed, why *did* he want to, is always a question, and one which he himself may not be able to answer. Health is a frequent deterrent in the approximately ten per cent of men who have never married. Dependency in the family; "I couldn't leave my parents or bring anyone into the family while they lived." "During my marrying years I was too busy getting started in my profession." "Getting clear of debt and saving up for a start delayed marriage for me." "I guess I was afraid. I had heard women were extravagant and would sell the shirt off your back." And, of course, there is the old lost love as well as the fear of women, especially among those men who have not known them at close range. Many men are not only afraid women will wreck them financially, but they are afraid of losing their freedom. "I like my own way of doing things." And, if truth were told, some of them are afraid of the sex side, afraid they might not be able to make the grade. This last group of men is usually made up of those who have lived morally, without irregularities, and have found their satisfactions in some sort of sublimation—their work, their philanthropies, or other interests outside the field of direct sex expression.

Today marriage is becoming more frequent in our country among both men and women, with an age extension which goes both up and down, back, that is, into the teens and forward into the later years of maturity. The intermingling of the sexes in business and the professions today, unlike the occupations of women in the past as milliners, teachers, and dressmakers whose work limited them to their own sex, is largely responsible. There is also the greater provision for elderly people in rest homes and hotels so that a son or daughter need not be asked to forego an earlier marriage. Then, too, more frequent and earlier dating on the part of young people tends to put boys and girls at their ease and to dispel fears long before the marriage age arrives. Last of all, or really first of all, there is sex education which permits the expression and acceptance of the sex impulse in children without leaving that residue of guilt and fear which in so many instances in the past has hindered the achievemen of marriage. Among my acquaintances are betrothed couples who have spent their lives faithfully devoted to each other, but have not been courageous enough to marry.

These four changes in our way of life are putting an end to celibacy in those men and women who because of circumstance or fear have been kept from marriage even though they were as ready and fitted for it as others who have attained it. In our concluding chapter I have a thought which may rescue these bachelors and maids if they wish to be rescued, but that remains to be not only seen but undertaken.

SUMMARY

As we finish this picture of the present-day outer fringe of family life, the future looks encouraging. Like the good old tallow candle on the kitchen shelf, always at hand to serve when the electric current fails, the older members of the family should be the ever-comforting reserve in times of household emergencies. The lure and the benefit of outside employment for young wives and mothers, to say nothing of the widowed and divorced, brings new and richer outlook to the older generation, lonely and eager for renewed family attachments.

Chapter XII

Forecast for the Future

THE last chapter of a book is usually a summary, a a gathering together of the threads of each chapter to tie them up crisply into a knot for handy use. This chapter, for example, should touch upon the growth stages of the sex impulse in childhood as it affects the adult marriage pattern, upon the progressive dating sequence through the adolescent years, upon the hard core of the engagement period as it faces realities, upon working wives and the social as well as the sexual by-products of women in industry, both before and after marriage.

Much more important and worth-while, I feel, is an interpretive and speculative look. What do we see in the future? What we see is bound to promote protests and disagreement from the men, but in the feminine quarter, if we are not mistaken, we shall hear smothered whoops of joy. We may even startle a few people into exclaiming, "No, no, it mustn't happen here!"

What we see cannot be supported by actual figures. The figures have been gathering like snowballs for a long time under trained observation by skilled writers and researchers in the marriage field. But figures are merely indications of present trends, and trends, like streams and rivers in a landscape, change from time to time. They go straight ahead or they take a turn or they merge with other streams, bringing in the end, if they continue, increased richness to the countryside, or, depending on their volume, they bring devastating flood. In making marriage history we hope for richness, not devastation. We hope for welfare through progress without detriment or danger of flood tide in hasty or precipitate action.

Marriage Is for Two has been based on trends observed from the kaleidoscope of the lives of men and women married, unmarried, separated, widowed, divorced who are part of the daily come and go in our separate nation-wide communities. They are the men and women, like you and me, who play out their marriage drama on everybody's doorstep while all the world looks on.

As they make up the composite marriage scene today, it may be interpreted only as one in swift transition, a reflection or result of a changing, tumultuous world. War and strife between countries do not calm nerves and bring harmony between individuals. Financial prosperity gained largely from technological pursuits does not foster creative and emotional bonds that hold men and women together. Nor does woman's growing economic efficiency leave her the secure "always there" wife and homemaker she was in the past.

Transition, not tradition, is the word that describes marriage today, and of the three forces—technology, financial prosperity, and the employment of women— the one that is serving most actively in the attainment of marriage, as well as in its more frequent disruption, is her own economic status—money in her pocket.

Girls and women have been quick to recognize the advantages this new earning power gives them and are making prompt use of it with the young teen-ager in the lead. Look what it has done for her and what she has done with it! She has been able to marry younger —at fifteen, sixteen, seventeen with or without her parents' consent. "Two can live more cheaply together than apart." It has made divorce easier and quicker when enemies to a continuing marriage have cropped up: disillusionment—"I didn't expect it to be like this"; vanishing romance—"He doesn't care the way he used to"; restlessness during the long stretches of the young husband's absence on business or military service— "He can't expect me to sit by myself forever." All of these and other immaturities are suffered by the early teen-age wife who is not ready for marriage and its responsibilities, rarely ready, psychologically, for the greatest of them all, pregnancy and the care of little children.

"Not all of us mess up our marriages," these young people say in their own defense, while we reply, knowing that hundreds and thousands of them do every day, "No, of course not 'all' of you, but your record is bad." [1]

As for the mature young women out of school and established in their own vocations, the marriage picture has also quickened and sharpened. These girls have their bank accounts, their steady employment. They can always keep up their end in marriage. In the come and go of unattached men, as well as those in a pussy-wants-a-corner exchange of married partners, women would be less than human if they did not make some move to further their heart's desire and find themselves mates. This, most certainly, they are already doing in large numbers, both adroitly and aggressively, with varying results.

Traditionally, woman sat on her doorstep hoping and waiting for her knight to ride up and whisk her away, willy-nilly. She had to wait, she had no worldly goods to offer. Moreover, she had no means of leaving her doorstep should the knight gallop by without her. Man's reward for taking on the full support of a wife and family was the right of choice in the marriage selection. That was only just.

We all know the history of wife barter—heads of cattle and all that—then the dowries, later on, down to the present, no dowries at all. Today women with their employment and bank accounts have again changed their status. They have something to offer but in their

[1] In 1953, 1,498,000 girls and 431,000 boys were married in their teens. In that year, too, 768,000 teen-age girls and 144,000 teen-age boys obtained divorces or annulments.

own right. It is not barter, they are no longer dependent upon either father or suitor. The money they earn is theirs. They may use it as they please. Some girls are using it traditionally to attract by the old route of personal adornment and feminine charm. Other girls are using theirs more overtly to further their social contacts and marriage prospects. "I have two tickets for the Ice Follies." "I have an extra seat for the game (or the races, or whatever)." Why not? Plenty of young men who are still getting under way would welcome this lightening of their dating expenses. Yet many would not, partly because they are conventional and would not be willing to yield their masculine prerogatives, and partly because they fear more serious involvements, and this they do not like.

Yet, in spite of much masculine resistance, women are moving forward into a new place. They are following up their financial gains with social gains, which include dating and courtship advantages. It is the logical to-be-expected course, and, at present, represents a current but unacknowledged usage, not among all women to be sure, but among all ages of women, some of them gracefully subtle and others disgracefully aggressive.

Men are still largely traditional, as we know, and yield less readily to change in this, as in all other matters. "I go once when they ask me," one young fellow said, "but not a second time if I think they are serious." "It is disgusting to me," an older man said (as you would expect him to), "and I never could be interested." Said another young fellow, "The trouble with girls is, they want to get serious. I like to date and hope to marry, but you date a girl once, we have fun. Then if you don't call her up for a second date within a week she calls *you* up and starts promoting a repeat. After the second date she is practically ready for the ring—or your pin."

This is the picture: a young fellow who is ready for companionship, but not ready for marriage, is afraid to date. Mothers tells me that young junior high-school girls start telephoning their sons before the boys have even begun to mature or have the slightest interest in them.

Beside the traditional right and prerogative of a man to choose his own wife and of a woman to be chosen, there are strong valid reasons for modifying these traditions and permitting women the equality of initiative when it comes to the matter of dating and courtship.

Yet merely annexing a husband for the sake of her own marriage security is not to any woman's liking. Her activities in her own behalf must be open and above board. She must be permitted full social acceptance, otherwise the game has lost its savor. Many older girls and also teen-agers refuse to compete with aggressive girls, merely on the basis of feminine dignity and pride—also out of consideration for the man in question. "It wouldn't be fair to him—to either of us." Moreover, where is love if one must pursue the available, merely for security? That psychological aspect of a woman-wooed man is a significant one. Now, when she crosses the bridge into his camp, she not only loses caste but she loses the privilege of being wooed for love. When courtship is rightfully woman's business, as it is man's business today, the whole situation will be cleared of its distastefulness. And don't think when it is her business that she won't do it with grace and finesse, for she has a way of her own that will never change. What men object to—scheming and aggressive pursuit—will have vanished because there will be no longer any need for it.

The gains from such equality to the individual and to society, in general, will be without limit. Need I enumerate them? For one, they will lessen teen-age marriages, 144,000 for boys, 768,000 for girls in 1953 as reported from the Office of Vital Statistics. Youthful, hasty, impulsive marriages have many causes: escape from home conditions and school attendance, repetition of parents' marriage, romantic violent attachments, but most conspicuously the pressure of competition, biological competition on the part of girls who see hundreds of other girls surging about them, boy-conscious, date-conscious, marriage-conscious, and marriage-intent yet with no recognized means of reaching their goal. Were the right of choice hers, she would be able to take time to be selective, instead of bargain hunting, and she would be able to find the one most suited to her fancy, for, like men, she would be in command of the situation.

Not only would a girl be able to wait to full maturity to marry, but that maturity would be her greatest asset. She would have developed the charm, the seasoned intelligence, the richness of personality which she did not have in the days of her first youth.

Once the rights of courtship have been acceptable to all, men and women impartially, we can prophesy a strangely unexpected clearance in the market place. Where, we shall ask, are the unmarrieds? Where are the mismated? Where are the teen-aged wives? Where are those who married for marriage's sake? Then, too, where are those wives who continue to live with husbands they do not love because of the social oblivion of a manless existence, to say nothing of those who feel the necessity to hold their men by the acceptance of illegitimate relationships?

The whole tradional courtship situation does not square with woman's present-day economic and educational status. Yet there are many, aside from the men, who will question the feasibility of any change in the status quo. They will feel that women have now all the initiative they can stand. They will shudder at the thought of girls let loose upon defenseless boys and men. The protests will arise that have always arisen when new pathways were opened up for women— against suffrage back in the 1920's, against women's employment during the 1940's. Yet the vote and the wage have not masculinized our women, and granting them a share in the choice of their lifelong mates certainly will not. It will only add to the many facets of modern woman's personality which already makes her the resourceful and surprising person she really is.

The trend toward a shared initiative in the association of men and women leading to marriage, is, it seems to me, one of the most promising and far-reaching in this transitional age. It will not be a sudden acquisition or one subject to legislation. It will be accomplished purely by social sanction, or lacking that, as in other progressive measures, by gradual, silent adoption and demonstration. This is an age of progress in international, racial, and sex equality. Let us hope that it will also be an age of progress and equality in the marriage field.

Index